Tales from the Tyne

Dick Keys and Ken Smith

RICHARD E. KEIS, 2006

Tyne Bridge Publishing

Acknowledgements

The authors would like to thank the following for their kind help in the preparation of this book: Brian Aitken, Editor, The Journal, Newcastle; Bob Balmer, of Blyth; Colin Boyd, of Newcastle; John Dobson, of Newcastle; Ron French, of Wooler; Adrian Osler, of Lesbury, Alnwick; Ray Marshall, Evening Chronicle; Newcastle Chronicle & Journal; Tyne & Wear Archives; Tyne & Wear Museums; the staffs of South Shields Library and Newcastle Libraries & Information Service.

Illustrations acknowledgements: unless otherwise indicated illustrations are reproduced from the collections of Newcastle Libraries & Information Service.

Published by
City of Newcastle upon Tyne
Newcastle Libraries & Information Service
Tyne Bridge Publishing
2006

www.tynebridgepublishing.co.uk

ISBN: 1 85795 158 1
978 185795 158 5

Printed by Elanders Hindson, North Tyneside

Front cover: the first *New Londoner*, c.1910. She served on the Newcastle-London passenger service.

Back cover: The pilot cutter *Queen o' the May* off the Coble Landing, South Shields, c.1932 (South Tyneside MBC).

Dick Keys is a retired merchant seaman, and keen maritime historian. Ken Smith is a sub-editor on The Journal, Newcastle. Dick Keys and Ken Smith are the authors of several books on the maritime history of the Tyne.

See www.tynebridgepublishing.co.uk for details, or contact Tyne Bridge Publishing, City Library, Princess Square, Newcastle upon Tyne, NE99 1DX, for a free catalogue.

Near the mouth of the Ouseburn, around 1950.

Contents

A 'puffer', possibly belonging to the Purdy Coal Co. of North Shields, makes her way upstream through Shields Harbour in the 1950s. Vessels like this were used to carry coal and other cargoes about the river.

Newcastle shore viewed from Gateshead, around 1830, engraved from a painting by J.W. Carmichael. Steam boats were in their infancy at this date and sail dominated river traffic.

From Newcastle Quay

In 1823 Joseph Shield, a Tyne shipping agent, had a new ship built on the South Shore, Gateshead, a 24-ton paddle steamer named the *Rapid*. She was a little over 63 feet long, 16 feet in breadth and specially fitted out with passenger accommodation.

Joseph Shield planned to use his new passenger steamer on a service from Newcastle to London, a route previously handled by sailing ships. He advertised that the *Rapid* would sail from Newcastle during the summer season for London every Monday, and from London for Newcastle every Thursday, with stops being made at Whitby, Scarborough and Great Yarmouth.

Richard E. Keys

An artist's impression of the paddle steamer Rapid.

STEAM CONVEYANCE TO LONDON.

THE RAPID, a FINE NEW STEAM VESSEL, FITTED OUT with EVERY ACCOMMODATION for PASSENGERS, will START from NEWCASTLE QUAY, on MONDAY MORNING, the 11TH of AUGUST, at NINE o'Clock; and LEAVE LONDON, at NINE o'Clock, on the THURSDAY FOLLOWING.

This Vessel will CONTINUE to RUN, during the SEASON, and will START every MONDAY MORNING, from NEWCASTLE, and every THURSDAY MORNING, from LONDON.

PASSENGERS LANDED at WHITBY, SCARBRO', or YARMOUTH.

Agents { JOS. SHIELD, Quayside, Newcastle. WM. & GEO. ANDREWS, 32, Trinity-Square, London.

At 5pm on 11 August 1823, the *Rapid* left Newcastle Quay. There were no problems with the down river run, but once clear of the Tyne Bar she ran slap into a howling south-westerly gale. Bravely the little steamer struggled southwards with London as her ultimate goal. However, a leak developed. Seventeen hours after her departure from Newcastle she was brought to a halt off Whitby and her captain decided all the passengers should be landed there for their own safety. The *Rapid* returned to the Tyne for repairs.

Joseph Shield postponed any further attempts to introduce steam power on the Newcastle-London run until spring the next year. Accordingly, the *Rapid* left Newcastle Quay at 8.40am on 17 May 1824 and berthed safely at London 54 hours later after a 'delightful passage'. Working against a headwind, the return run took 60 hours, but she kept to the

advertised schedule, arriving back in the Tyne at 4am on 24 May and leaving for London again later the same day.

Travellers from the North-East had been given a taste of what steamships had to offer. The *Newcastle Courant* declared in the flowery language of the time that the service 'will prove a most convenient mode of communication with the Metropolis, not only for passengers but for the conveyance of goods requiring dispatch'.

Despite the plaudits, Shield's pioneering Newcastle-London steamer service did not last long. In April 1825 it was reported that the *Rapid* had been sold for 'coral fishery' work off the Algerian coast.

However, steam power for passengers returned to the route in 1827 when the tall-funnelled paddle steamer *Hylton Jolliffe* entered service between London and Newcastle. The 340-ton ship belonged to the General Steam Navigation Company, a London-based business. She had accommodation

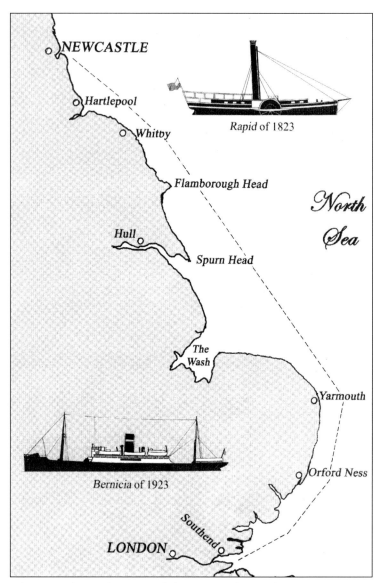

This map shows the route of the Newcastle-London steamers down the East Coast. The service lasted over a century. The Rapid of 1823 was the first steamer to link Newcastle and London and one of the last was the Bernicia of 1923.

The only alternative to sea travel was a lengthy journey by stage coach until the advent of the railways.

for about 50 passengers. Somewhat ironically, her Newcastle agent was Joseph Shield, the former owner of the *Rapid*.

The *Hylton Jolliffe* arrived in the Tyne on the morning of 7 June 1827. She left the following day and arrived in London on the morning of 10 June after a passage along the East Coast lasting just over 40 hours.

The passengers were reported to be 'all delighted with the trip, not having felt the slightest inconvenience of sea sickness and expressed themselves highly satisfied with the comfort and accommodation afforded in this fine vessel'. A couple of months later the *Hylton Jolliffe* steamed from London to Newcastle in only 35 and a half hours. This was claimed to be the quickest passage made on the route up until that date.

The General Steam Navigation Company of London later placed other steamships on the successful service, including the *Tourist, City of Hamburgh, London Merchant, Neptune* and *Dragon*.

Steamers had come to stay. Initially, they only operated a summer service, but as confidence grew in the reliability of their engines, this was extended to cover the whole year. They were soon to cream off much of the passenger and light goods trade, not only from the sailing ships, but also from horse and coach travel on land.

Even when the service was interrupted by weather, the steamships could still beat the London stage coaches. In May 1830 it was reported that the steamer *Tourist* had been unable to sail from Newcastle for three days because of a severe gale and many of her passengers had decided to switch to land travel. On the fourth day the *Tourist* was at last able to depart the Tyne and arrived in the capital several hours before those who had travelled by coach.

London's General Steam Navigation Company had the monopoly of the Newcastle to London steamer trade until 1853 when the pioneering steam collier *John Bowes* entered the stakes. This iron-hulled vessel was driven by a propeller (screw) instead of paddles.

Launched and completed by Palmers of Jarrow the previous year, the *John Bowes* had been built specifically for the coal trade from the Tyne to London, but she was having legal

STEAM BETWEEN NEW-CASTLE AND LONDON.—ONCE A WEEK.—The New Iron Screw Steamer VOLUNTEER, (Captain HOSSACK), now running, (Weather permitting), sails from Newcastle every Wednesday Morning, and returns from Irongate Wharf, London, every Saturday Evening, carrying Goods at moderate Rates of Freight.

This Vessel is registered 312 Tons, and is constructed with 'tween Decks and every Appliance requisite for the careful Stowage and Transit of Goods between Newcastle and London, for which Trade she has been expressly built by the Owners, who respectfully solicit the Support of the Community.

DUNCAN ROBERTSON, Agent,
Irongate Wharf, London; and
WM. LAING & CO. General Shipping Agency
Office, New Quay, Newcastle.

problems. Her steam power represented a challenge to the sailing colliers which lacked her speed and regularity. An Act of Parliament prevented her from 'jumping' the queue of sailing vessels at the staiths (loading jetties) in the Tyne and her owners decided to seek alternative employment for her. Accordingly, she was placed on a regular cargo service between Newcastle and London, starting in March 1853. The ship was managed by William Laing, Junior, & Company, of Newcastle.

By August, the *John Bowes* had been joined by another iron screw steamer, the *Chanticleer*, which was 'splendidly fitted' with accommodation for passengers. However, it was not long before this new service was experiencing difficulties. The problem was at the London end. Getting these comparatively large vessels discharged was taking much longer than anticipated and by mid-September William Laing announced that the service would have to be abandoned.

The venture had been a failure, but Laing did not drop the idea of a steamer service from the Tyne to the Thames. In January 1854 he announced that the 'large and powerful first class steamship' *Monarch*, which he had chartered at 'considerable expense', would run a goods-only service until the spring when his new iron screw steamship, the *Volunteer*, was expected to be ready for service. The vessel was then being built by Palmers shipyard at Jarrow.

Right, on cue, the *Volunteer* entered service in late April. But before the ship had time to really settle down on the London run she was taken up by the government to carry supplies to British forces in the Crimea. War with Russia had been declared on 28 March 1854.

Despite this interruption, William Laing, and his partner, William Davies Stephens (better known as W.D. Stephens, a

From Ward's Directory, 1858. Lifeguard, Brigadier and Volunteer are shown as the steamers on the Newcastle-London run.

prominent alderman and mayor of Newcastle), persevered. Six months after the *Volunteer* had entered service another new, Jarrow-built steamer, the *Champion*, made her debut. In turn, she was followed by the *Brigadier*, *Sentinel*, *Admiral*, *Lifeguard* and *Dragoon*.

Shipping businessman, W.D. Stephens.

In 1862 Laing withdrew from his partnership with Stephens, but became involved in the shipping trade between the Tyne and Leith. Stephens continued to run the Newcastle-London service until 1864 when he amalgamated his fleet with those of two other businesses to form the Tyne Steam Shipping Company. It was to prove a great success. In 1903 this firm merged with three other concerns to form the Tyne-Tees Steam Shipping Company and this too enjoyed considerable custom.

The names of the Newcastle-London passenger boats of the Tyne Steam Shipping Company and its successor the Tyne-Tees Steam Shipping Company became household words to many people on the North-East coast – *Tynesider*, *Londoner*, the two *New Londoners*, *Royal Dane*, *John Ormston*, *Stephen Furness*, *Richard Welford*, and last, but not least, *Bernicia* and *Hadrian*. The service did not close until 1934, 101 years after the little paddle steamer *Rapid* had first ventured southwards from the Tyne.

STEAM TO HULL.

THE STEAMER NEPTUNE,

(CAPTAIN WILLIAM ELLIOTT),

Leaves Newcastle every Saturday (weather permitting)

Two Hours before High Water, and

Leaves Hull every Wednesday.

☞ FREIGHTS VERY MODERATE.

FARES—BEST CABIN, 6s.; SECOND DITTO, 4s.,

Steward's Fee included.

AGENTS—W. L. MURES, North Shore, Newcastle; T. F. BELL & Co., Hull.

Tyne and Continental Steam Navigation Company, Newcastle-on-Tyne.

STEAMERS

FOR HAMBURG, TWICE A-WEEK.

FOR ROTTERDAM, ONCE A-WEEK.

FOR STETTIN AND ST. PETERSBURG, DURING THE SEASON.

☞ *See Advertisements.*

ORMSTON, DOBSON & CO., AGENTS.

NORTH SHORE.

WARD'S NORTH OF ENGLAND POCKET BOOKS,

Being compiled expressly for the District are therefore doubly valuable.

Many steam ship companies operated from the Tyne. This advertisement is from an 1861-62 directory.

Hadrian is launched on 15 March 1923 at the Wallsend shipyard of Swan Hunter and Wigham Richardson. She was one of the last Newcastle-London steamers.

Steamers and captains

The Tyne Steam Shipping Company's steamers were a familiar sight at Newcastle Quay in the late 19th century and became an enduring feature of the river. Among the most favourite boats was the *Royal Dane*, built for the firm's relatively short-lived service from the Tyne to Copenhagen and then placed on the Newcastle-London run in 1877.

A contributor to the *Newcastle Examiner* declared in 1884: 'The Tyne Steam Shipping Company's steamer *Royal Dane* is one of the best passenger ships sailing from the Tyne. Her great length, together with the grip she takes of the water when fairly laden, make her a capital sea boat, even in rough weather, and she rolls very little – the motion so fatal to so many unfortunate landsmen when they 'go down to the sea in ships'.

'The saloons and cabins are placed near the deck level, and as a consequence the air is always fresh and plentiful. The *Royal Dane* has been recently fitted with the electric light and this has tended to the further sweetening of the atmosphere on board. When we crossed the bar on Saturday afternoon about one o'clock there was a considerable breeze blowing from the east, but only one of the passengers was affected with sea sickness in a serious form – the bulk of the passengers remained on deck until dark.'

The writer for the *Examiner* was full of praise for the passenger facilities and crew: 'Nothing can exceed the clean-

GENERAL REFRESHMENT TARIFF.

Victualling in the Company's Steamers is not compulsory upon Passengers, with the exception that in the Foreign Trades Saloon Dinner is charged for. Stewards' Fees are included in the Fares.

Refreshments are provided on board all the Company's Steamers as per the subjoined Tariff. In the London Trade, Passengers have the option of making a contract for the journey, such option to be declared before sailing. If by contract, the charges will be:—In the Saloon, 6s.; in the Fore Cabin, 3s., subject to the following conditions:—When the Vessel sails within an hour before Dinner time, no Dinner will be served that day. If ordered, it will be charged according to Tariff. Meals served before departure or after arrival will be charged per Tariff.

Meal Times—Breakfast, 8·30 a.m.; Dinner, 1·30 p.m.; Tea, 6·0 p.m.

		Saloon Price.	Fore Cabin Price.
Breakfast, with Meat or Fish, as per Menu... each		2s. 0d.	1s. 0d.
,, Plain ,,		1s. 0d.	0s. 9d.
Luncheons ,,		1s. 0d.	0s. 9d.
Dinners, as per Menu ... ,,		2s. 6d.	1s. 0d.
Teas do. ,,		2s. 0d.	1s. 0d.
,, Plain ,,		1s. 0d.	0s. 9d.
Suppers ... ,,		1s. 0d.	0s. 9d.
Grilled Chop or Steak ... ,,		1s. 3d.	1s. 0d.
Plate of Meat and Bread ... ,,		1s. 0d.	9d. or 6d.
Sandwiches (Ham or Tongue) ,,		0s. 4d.	4d. or 2d.
Tea or Coffee specially made, in Pots ,,		0s. 6d.	0s. 4d.
Cup of Tea, Coffee, or Cocoa ,,		0s. 3d.	0s. 3d.
,, ,, ,, with Bread and Butter... ,,		0s. 6d.	0s. 6d.
Cup of Bovril or Bouillon Fleet		0s. 3d.	0s. 3d.
Bread and Cheese ... Plate		0s. 4d.	0s. 3d.
Soup ... Basin		1s. 0d.	0s. 3d.
,, ... Plate		0s. 6d.	0s. 3d.
Ice Cream ... Glass		0s. 2d.	0s. 2d.
Jelly ...			
Champagne ... Pint Bottle		4s. 0d.	4s. 0d.
Port or Sherry ... ,, ,,		2s. 6d.	2s. 6d.
,, ,, ... Glass		0s. 6d.	0s. 6d.
Claret ... Pint Bottle		1s. 6d.	1s. 6d.
Ale and Stout ... ,,		0s. 6d.	0s. 6d.
Lemonade, Ginger Beer, and Soda Water ... ,,		0s. 3d.	0s. 2d.
Nectar Cream Beverages.—Orange, Lemon, Cherry, Raspberry, Ginger, Aromatic, Burtonia, or Kola	per Half Pint Bottle	0s. 3d.	0s. 2d.
	per Champagne Pint Bottle	0s. 4d.	0s. 4d.

A menu typical of the Tyne-Tees ships.

liness of the saloons and cabins of the *Royal Dane*, and that passenger must be very exacting who can find fault with the attention paid to his comfort and convenience by Mr George Isbister and Mrs Milburn, the chief steward and stewardess of the *Royal Dane*.'

The electric lights aboard the vessel had evidently suffered from a little problem. The writer reported: 'On Saturday night there was a slight hitch or two with the light, but on Sunday evening it burned most brilliantly up to the time of mooring the ship in the Thames at midnight. The Siemen's engine is driven at great speed and is liable to get heated.'

However, the writer added: 'The slight hitches which occurred on Saturday night arose from causes which can be easily dealt with and I am bound to state here that the electric lighting of the *Royal Dane* is a complete success, and that it adds much to the pleasure and comfort of the passengers.' In another contemporary account, a passenger pointed out that electric lights did away with the smell of oil in the saloons and cabins.

On a different voyage to London in the same year the *Royal Dane*, which could keep up an average speed of 12 knots, outpaced the *General Havelock*, a Sunderland passenger steamer, also bound for the capital.

The master of the *Royal Dane* in 1884 was Captain John Cracknell, who was one of the best-known of the company's captains. He must have been as familiar a sight at Newcastle Quay as the various steamers he commanded over a long career.

John Cracknell was a seaman of great experience and eventually became commodore of the Tyne Steam Shipping Company's fleet. During 39 years of service he made the voyage from the Tyne to London and back over 3,500 times and his ships were estimated to have carried around 250,000 passengers during that time. Also during that time he commanded most of the company's vessels.

Cracknell first went to sea as a cabin boy on a sailing vessel at the age of nine and rose through the ranks as seaman, mate and master. He became a captain at the relatively young age of 25. While in command of his first ship Captain Cracknell sailed into the Tyne in a very heavy gale. The Tyne Bar was a maelstrom of broken water and he was greeted by the sight of 35 ships lying wrecked on the Black Middens rocks and Herd Sand.

The young mariner was soon commanding Newcastle-London steamers. The run from Newcastle Quay to the Wapping area of London took more than 30 hours in the 1860s. But by the late 1880s this time had been considerably reduced. Captain Cracknell's best run by the early 1890s was said to be 22 hours, achieved in the *Tynesider*. This was regarded as a considerable feat. The *Tynesider* had been completed by the Schlesinger Davis shipyard at Wallsend in 1888.

While in command of the Tyne Steam Shipping Company's *Grenadier* in September 1883 Captain Cracknell encountered a very heavy gale and became anxious over the situation as he paced the bridge. He remained worried throughout the night, but when dawn broke he went to lie down on his couch in the chart-room for a brief rest. Cracknell then fell asleep and dreamt he saw a steamer struggling through a fierce storm. He recognised the vessel as the *Inchclutha* which was commanded by his eldest son George, whose figure he could make out on the bridge.

Cracknell then saw a huge wave come rushing down upon

the ship, completely covering the stern. Before the vessel could recover, a second wave, greater than the first, crashed over her and she sank. Captain Cracknell awoke with a start and rushed up to the bridge. Highly distressed, he told the mate his son had been drowned. No trace of the ship was ever found. The ill-fated *Inchclutha* had been built on the Tyne at Charles Mitchell's Low Walker Yard, being completed in 1879. The captain's dream of tragedy may be regarded by some as a psychic experience.

The steamship Tynesider is dwarfed by the great Mauretania being fitted out at Wallsend in 1907. Crowds of people on the Tynesider's foredeck are admiring the liner.

There were, of course, also many light moments in this well-liked seaman's career. Concerts were often held aboard the Newcastle-London boats, with passengers and sometimes stewards or stewardesses taking part. In an age without television, CDs, DVDs or disco music people organised their own live entertainment, with the ship's piano often providing the accompaniment to the singing. Recitals of poems and excerpts from plays seem also to have been popular.

An observer writing in the *Northern Weekly Leader* in the late 1880s tells us of the aftermath of one such concert, aboard the *Tynesider* with Captain Cracknell in command: 'The official programme was exhausted at 10 o'clock. There was an adjournment up on deck and on the leeside an impromptu sing-song of glees and solos proceeded for a couple of hours.

'The vocalists before retiring resolved to serenade the captain and surrounding his stateroom on deck, the tenor and soprano warbled: 'Sleeper awake, bright stars are beaming' – when the dry but expressive cough of the commodore was heard to windward. A rush was made and then it was found that the serenade had been made to an empty berth, for there he was spinning a yarn among the ladies while keeping his weather eye open on the progress of his ship. He joined in *Auld Lang Syne* and then everybody retired for the night.'

The following morning the *Tynesider* was steaming up the Thames and berthed before 11am at the Free Trade Wharf, Ratcliff, close to Stepney, after a passage from Newcastle Quay lasting 24 and a half hours.

A writer for the *Young Men's Magazine* who left Newcastle Quay aboard the *Juno* in 1889 wrote: 'It is a very pleasant custom on board the London and Tyne boats to hold a concert if possible during the evening, and this voyage proved no exception. Captain Little was voted to the chair and about 60 people attended.

'A capital programme of 15 pieces was gone through to the evident satisfaction of all. Mr Isbister, one of the stewards, proved to be quite a host in himself, reciting with much verve two scenes from *The Merchant of Venice* and *Othello*. The young lady who presided at the piano also rendered efficient service. The collecting box was sent round and ten shillings was realised for the widows and orphans of the Shipwrecked Mariners' Fund.'

The *Juno* reached the wharf in London the following afternoon after a trip of 26 and three quarter hours.

Captain Thomas Little was among the other well-known masters in the service of the Tyne Steam Shipping Company. He was said to be of a 'kindly, unassuming disposition'. Also well remembered was Captain Alexander Cay, from Peterhead, who served for many years with the company and suffered from poor hearing because of 'prolonged immersion in water' after one of his ships was sunk.

Another veteran was Captain J.W.N. Searle who had four sons and four daughters. Originally from Kent, he began sailing from the Tyne as an able seaman and became one of the company's captains in 1873. An observer described him as 'a gentlemanly specimen with his fine uniform, patent leather shoes and gloves' and 'for the time the trip lasts a regular father to the large and varied family of passengers'. Captain Searle died on Tyneside – at his home in Gateshead in 1905 at the age of 70.

The service from Newcastle seems to have been generally well organised, but occasionally things went wrong. For example, on a Saturday afternoon in June 1902, the *New Londoner* was besieged by would-be passengers prior to her departure at Newcastle Quay. It was a chaotic scene.

Captain J.W.N. Searle, engraved from a photograph for his obituary, 1905.

The steamer was fully booked with her maximum number of 211 berth passengers, but far more people turned out on the day because tickets had been sold in excess of this number. It became clear there were simply too many passengers and the result was that a huge crowd made a rush to board the ship.

Half an hour before the *New Londoner* was due to sail the gangways were cast off and it was reported that husbands were parted from their wives and parents from their children. One father slipped ashore to buy some fruit for his family and was unable to return. Other people saw their luggage sail away down the Tyne as the *New Londoner* headed outward bound for the Thames. The vessel was carrying 480 passengers. It was said to be the most she had ever taken aboard. Ironically, some of those left behind had booked their passage weeks ahead. They could not have been amused.

In 1931 a couple living in the South-East of England decided to take a short pleasure cruise aboard the steamer *Britannia* from Southend to the *Nore* Lightship. It was a lovely summer's day. They boarded a ship lying at the pier and settled themselves down on deck, preparing to spend a pleasant hour or so at sea.

Unfortunately, they were to spend more than 24 hours on what was the wrong ship. The vessel duly sailed away from the Thames Estuary into the North Sea. They remarked to one of the steamer's officers that it was an excellent trip and very good value for money at one shilling and sixpence considering the distance travelled.

It was only then that the couple discovered they were aboard the Tyne Tees Steam Shipping Company's *Bernicia* and were on their way to Newcastle, nearly 300 miles away. The *Bernicia* had called at Southend to pick up passengers.

The couple had to go all the way to Newcastle. When they reached the Tyne they were faced with the problem of getting back to London as they were carrying little cash.

Bernicia steams up the Tyne on her trials, 12 July 1923.

They went to the railway and coach companies and later the police. Finally, it was agreed they would have to wait in Newcastle until money was sent to them from London. The two passengers from the South had experienced a truly surprise trip to the canny city on the Tyne.

From the North Mail 27 July 1923:

'A party of 111 North Country boys and girls from the Royal Merchant Seamen's Orphanage at Wokingham, Berkshire, arrived at Newcastle Quay last night aboard the Bernicia on their way to spend the summer holidays with relatives. Every year the Tyne Tees S.S. Co. provides a free passage for the children from London to Newcastle and back.'

Bound for the Cup Final

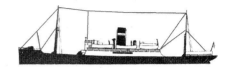

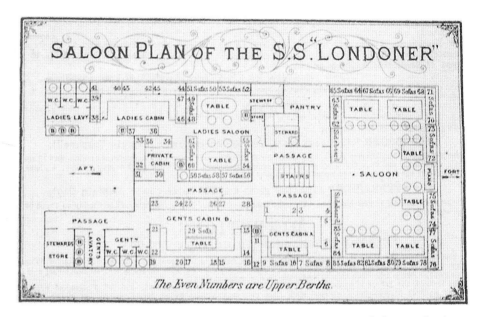

SALOON PLAN OF THE S.S. "LONDONER"

The Even Numbers are Upper Berths.

On the morning of 17 February 1878 the Tyne Steam Shipping Company's *CM Palmer* was sunk in collision with another vessel while on her way from Newcastle to London. Fourteen people aboard the *CM Palmer* lost their lives – nine passengers and five of the crew.

The *CM Palmer* had been hit amidships by the steamer *Ludworth* during thick fog near the mouth of the Thames and slipped beneath the waves within ten minutes. Many people jumped overboard from the Tyne ship after the impact and steam blown off from the side of the vessel was believed to have scalded some of them to death. Fortunately, 43 people were rescued from the water by the *Ludworth*'s two boats.

The *CM Palmer* had been one of the finest vessels in the service of the Tyne Steam Shipping Company at this period. She was completed by Palmers shipyard at Jarrow in 1870 and was appropriately named after the famed businessman Charles Mark Palmer, the founder of the shipyard who was also chairman of Tyne Steam Shipping.

At the time of the accident the ship was commanded by Captain Alexander Cay, who is said to have remained standing by the wheel until the last moments before his vessel sank. He was exonerated of any blame for the collision.

However, Captain Cay was to see a second ship under his command sunk. In 1893 another of the company's Newcastle-London ships was lost. On 14 May that year the *Londoner* sank in the North Sea, about 20 miles from Great Yarmouth, after being struck by a large steamer, the *Sheffield*, again during thick fog. The *Londoner* had been carrying about 90 passengers. Those travellers having breakfast in the *Londoner*'s saloon were able to see daylight through the hole punched in the side of their ship.

Two boats with women and children got away from the *Londoner* and the crew of the *Sheffield* also launched their boats to help in the rescue. However, the *Sheffield* had been damaged and the passengers and crew were transferred to the steamers *Ashton, City of Aberdeen*, the collier *Boston*, the warship HMS *Bulldog*, and a tug which had arrived on the scene.

All passengers and crew survived, except for an unfortunate Italian man named Ambro Zoli, a hotel proprietor at Shields, who was badly injured and died later in hospital. He had been accompanied by his wife, who survived. Many of the passengers were landed at Grimsby and some at North Shields.

The *Londoner* was another Tyne-built vessel. She had been completed by the Schlesinger Davis shipyard at Wallsend in 1891, and was a sister ship of the *Tynesider*, which also served on the Newcastle-London run.

Captain Cay was in command of the *Londoner* at the time of the collision and he was again cleared of any blame at the subsequent Board of Trade Inquiry. He must have felt that to have two ships sunk during a career as a captain was more than enough.

The *New Londoner* was completed at Wigham Richardson's Neptune Yard, Low Walker, Newcastle, in 1894 as a replacement for the lost ship. She was sold in 1911 and the following year a second *New Londoner* began service on the route.

The outbreak of the First World War in 1914 led to further losses of company vessels, by then relaunched under the name Tyne-Tees Steam Shipping Co. The first casualty was the *Sir William Stephenson*. On 29 August 1915 she struck a mine off Great Yarmouth while on her way from the Tyne to London with general cargo. The vessel was taken in tow but went down in Yarmouth Roads. Two men lost their lives.

More was to come. On 5 October 1915 the newly-built steamer *Novocastrian* struck a mine off Lowestoft while on passage from London to Newcastle. She went down after a career lasting only a few months.

The *Novocastrian* had been launched at S.P. Austin & Son's yard, Sunderland, in February that year. The captain of the ship at the time of the sinking was John Bruce, who

The first New Londoner. The back of this postcard which was mailed 11 September 1910 reads: 'Behold me here among the crowd! Beware that you never come by the "New Londoner" – she is a horrid boat with small cabins that harbour cockroaches! Your hamper was most appreciated but I felt very ill and only managed one egg … the sea was grand but too rough to be comfortable, it bounced me about terribly!'

served in the company's vessels for 42 years. During his career Captain Bruce was said to have carried around 300,000 passengers and 2 million tons of cargo on voyages between the Tyne and London and 15,000 passengers and 1 million tons of cargo on the company's runs to Continental ports such as Rotterdam, Hamburg and Antwerp.

One crew member, engineer William Wake Paddon, survived the sinking of both the *Sir William Stephenson* and the *Novocastrian*. He rose to become the company's marine superintendent engineer.

The *Grenadier*, a former Newcastle-London service ship, was sunk on 23 February 1917 when she struck a mine, again laid by a U-boat, near the Shipwash Light Vessel, near Orfordness, Suffolk, while on passage from Rotterdam to the Tyne. Eight lives were lost.

The *Juno* was also unlucky, but survived the war. She was detained in Hamburg at the outbreak of hostilities in 1914. Her crew were interned until the Armistice of 1918. However, the vessel never returned to the service of Tyne-Tees Steam Shipping Co., although she served under various foreign flags until broken up in 1935.

Isabella Crammond, of Whitley Bay, served as a stewardess aboard Tyne-Tees ships for much of the First World War, running from the Tyne and Wear to London and the Continent. She recalled 'eerie' nights when the steamers would creep along the East Coast with all lights out as at any moment disaster could come in the shape of torpedoes or mines. One night did, indeed, bring an ordeal. The *Grenadier* lost her anchors in a severe storm and was driven ashore at Gorleston, near Great Yarmouth, between two other wrecked ships. When morning broke Isabella was rescued by breaches buoy.

The *Grenadier* had been fortunate. Daylight also revealed five mines on the beach. The vessel had grounded on sand and soon she was refloated and taken into port by a pilot for examination. The stewardess rejoined her ship. Captain Aubin had come to regard Isabella as the ship's lucky mascot.

On the next voyage, the *Grenadier* struck a mine and Captain Aubin and seven crew were lost. But Isabella was not aboard. In the last months of the war the stewardess worked on munitions at the Elswick Works, Newcastle.

Isabella Crammond, with her medals, pictured in a local newspaper on 30 January, 1939.

Tyne-Tees Steam Shipping resumed its Newcastle-London service after the First World War with the vessel *Richard Welford* which had been refitted after war service as an armed boarding vessel. On 13 August 1919 she sailed from Newcastle Quay for the Free Trade Wharf in London.

In 1923 the new ships *Bernicia* and *Hadrian* entered service on the route. The *Bernicia* had been built at Hawthorn Leslie's Hebburn Yard and the *Hadrian* by Swan Hunter &

WEMBLEY
CUP FINAL

MAKE THE
TYNE-TEES STEAMER
YOUR
HOTEL.

SPECIALLY REDUCED FARES.

Why not make your trip to the Cup Final a pleasant holiday for four days at little cost?

Leave **NEWCASTLE QUAY** by the s.s. "Bernicia," at 10 p.m., on WEDNESDAY, 20th APRIL.

Return from Free Trade Wharf, London, at midnight on SATURDAY, 23rd April.

RETURN FARE 25s. (First Class).

Sleep on board the steamer in comfort while in London, two nights at 2/6 per night. You will have two delightful days sailing on the coast, two glorious days in London, for a cost of 30/- for fare and accommodation. Meals and refreshments can be obtained on board at reasonable prices. Second class return fare **15/-**, excluding accommodation on board in London.

Apply—**TYNE-TEES STEAM SHIPPING Co. Ld.,**
25, KING STREET,
Telephone 23111.   **NEWCASTLE-ON-TYNE.**

Gail & Sons, Printers, 29 & 31, Quayside, Newcastle-on-Tyne.

A poster advertises the 1932 Cup Final. The Bernicia acted as a floating hotel.

Wigham Richardson at Wallsend. They were to be the last of the company's vessels to run on the passenger service between Newcastle and London.

Except in stormy weather, many people evidently found a trip to the capital by steamer both relaxing and enjoyable. Best remembered were the voyages to see Newcastle United play in the FA Cup Final.

The company used their 'fine steamer' the *New Londoner* for the trip to see the 1905 Final and it was reported that more than 100 Newcastle supporters took the opportunity to travel by sea. Unfortunately, their team lost 2-0 to Aston Villa on this occasion.

Newcastle, however, were to be victorious following the First World War. The newly-built *Bernicia* carried fans to the Cup Final of 1924 in which Newcastle beat Aston Villa 2-0 before a crowd of 91,000 at Wembley Stadium. On the evening of 23 April the ship left Newcastle Quay with over 300 fans, her accommodation being fully booked. After she pulled away amid cheering, sirens and blowing of kisses from the shore, the Tyneside Highland Pipe Band, which had previously marched through the streets of the city, assembled on the bridge and played a spirited rendition of *Cock of the North*. The pipers later transferred to the tug *Titan* which led the way as the *Bernicia* sailed down the Tyne

A flag bearing a magpie on a white background fluttered from the *Bernicia*'s foremast with the words: 'United's f'th' Final'. It was noted at the time that a large number of women were among the supporters aboard.

At Jarrow and other places along the river, crowds cheered the fans on deck and they excitedly cheered back, confident of a Newcastle victory. Moored ships and tugs sounded their sirens. The *Bernicia* replied with her whistle.

Newcastle Chronicle & Journal Ltd.

Cup fever. Crowds pack the London Wharf, Newcastle Quayside, to cheer off the Bernicia on her way with a host of fans to the FA Cup Final in April 1924.

Ship launches were a way of life on the Tyne. Here, the launch party and guests for the passenger steamer Bernicia gather at the bow of the ship at the Hawthorn Leslie Yard, Hebburn on 1 May 1923. Hats are very much in evidence.

A lady prepares to christen the Bernicia, champagne at the ready.

Bernicia's smoking room, showing a wealth of woodwork.

The first class dining room aboard Bernicia.

A spartan-looking first class cabin on Bernicia. There was little luxury for the one-night passage.

The same ship also carried Newcastle United supporters to the 1932 Cup Final. It was reported that around 40,000 people, many of them singing, assembled on the city's quayside as the *Bernicia* prepared to sail on the evening of 20 April.

The first-class fare was 25 shillings return and passengers were able to use the ship as a hotel while moored at the Free Trade Wharf in London for an extra two shillings and sixpence per night.

The *Bernicia* was carrying a six foot high black and white replica of the FA Cup on her funnel. Passing ships signalled 'Good luck' – it seems a considerable number of captains were Newcastle supporters, including *Bernicia*'s Captain A.A. Lawrence.

More than 300 fans made the trip to see their team play at Wembley. They came home in triumph. Before a vast crowd of 92,000, Newcastle beat Arsenal 2-1.

The 1932 Final was to prove the last for the Newcastle-London boats. By 1929 the number of passengers on ordinary sailings was declining. The chairman of Tyne-Tees Steam Shipping, Sir Arthur Munro Sutherland, told the annual general meeting in 1929 that the buses had 'cut very heavily' into the company's passenger trade and they had been forced to reduce their fares. The running costs of the vessels and their crews meant that it was very doubtful whether the carrying of passengers could be continued.

In 1932 the *Hadrian* and *Bernicia* were laid up for the winter period and the *Alnwick* and *Newminster* were used on the route. These vessels carried fewer passengers. The *Alnwick* had been completed by Swan Hunter & Wigham Richardson at Wallsend in 1928.

The summer of 1934 was the last time passenger ships ran on the Newcastle-London service. After being laid up at Dunston at the end of the summer, the *Bernicia* was sold to Greek owners for £30,000. Her cost had been £80,000 when completed in 1923. The *Hadrian* was sold for around £31,500 to an Egyptian shipping company. It was the end of a long-lived service from Newcastle Quay, which today we call the Quayside.

The impressive, narrow stone building which housed the offices of the shipping company still stands on the corner of King Street with its frontage facing the Quayside and is now part of an Italian restaurant. The exterior bears a restored wooden plaque detailing the destinations to which the company's vessels sailed, a reminder of shipping days long since vanished.

Tugs on Tyne

The first steam vessel to be built on the Tyne is generally believed to be the *Tyne Steam Packet* which was launched from the South Shore, Gateshead, in February 1814. She caused quite a stir when she began a passenger service between Newcastle and Shields in the summer of that year and soon she was joined by a sister vessel. However, the service failed to attract enough business and folded after two years.

These wooden-hulled paddle steamers were then purchased by a Joseph Price of Gateshead, who renamed the *Tyne Steam Packet* the *Perseverance*. The other vessel was christened the *Eagle*. Price also tried to use them for a passenger service on the river, but again the venture failed.

Faced with a financial headache, he came up with the idea that he might be able to employ his steam boats to tow sailing ships in and out of the Tyne. The idea was to prove

The first Tyne tug, Perseverance, tows a brig up the river. Pictured in Smith's Dock Journal, 1933.

highly successful and began the era of tug boats on the river, setting an example to other ports around Britain.

Price approached shipowner Robert Robson, of Newcastle, and asked if he could try out his idea. Robson agreed. In July, 1818, the loaded sailing vessel *Friends Adventure* was towed down the Tyne to the sea by the *Perseverance*. It was claimed to be the first steam tow on record.

Joseph Price later wrote: 'I gave notice to Captain Copeland of the *Friends Adventure*, Hull trader, to have all ready from an hour to an hour and a half before high water. At the time appointed I requested him to throw a line on board the steamer.

'The tide was against us for the first three miles. Everything answered as well as I could wish, and the vessel was towed two miles over the bar in two hours and ten minutes – a distance of 13 miles, the wind against us all the way. This was the first time a sailing vessel was ever towed by a steamboat.'

Price met initial opposition to his venture from more conservative shipowners and captains but he continued with his towage business using the *Perseverance* and the *Eagle*. His persistence set an example to others, for three years after the first tow the number of wooden paddle tugs on the river had increased to 14.

The advantages of steam towage were too great to ignore. Sailing ships were now able to move up and down the river without needing to rely on favourable winds or tides. It was said that vessels, mainly colliers, which had previously averaged only eight voyages a year between the Tyne and Thames, now averaged 13. It is also claimed that other British ports took their lead from the Tyne in adopting steam tugs. This may well be true. Hull, Sunderland and Liverpool were among those reported to have followed in the wake of the Tyne initiative.

It seems, however, that in the early years on the river the paddle tugs had to supplement their income by sometimes acting as passenger steamers plying between Newcastle and Shields or taking people on pleasure trips. But with the growth of the Tyne as a major port the tug business was to become a full-time service.

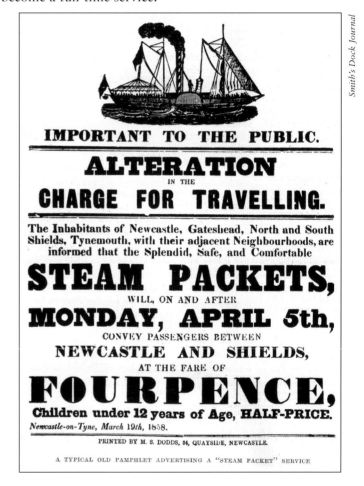

IMPORTANT TO THE PUBLIC.

ALTERATION
IN THE
CHARGE FOR TRAVELLING.

The Inhabitants of Newcastle, Gateshead, North and South Shields, Tynemouth, with their adjacent Neighbourhoods, are informed that the Splendid, Safe, and Comfortable

STEAM PACKETS,
WILL, ON AND AFTER
MONDAY, APRIL 5th,
CONVEY PASSENGERS BETWEEN
NEWCASTLE AND SHIELDS,
AT THE FARE OF
FOURPENCE,
Children under 12 years of Age, HALF-PRICE.

Newcastle-on-Tyne, March 19th, 1858.

PRINTED BY M. S. DODDS, 54, QUAYSIDE, NEWCASTLE.

A TYPICAL OLD PAMPHLET ADVERTISING A "STEAM PACKET" SERVICE

Smith's Dock Journal

The paddle tug President, which helped escort the famous Tyne passenger liner Mauretania down the river for her delivery voyage in October 1907.

Numerous tugs, both paddle and screw driven, were to be built on the banks of the river. The shipyards of J.P. Rennoldson, J.T. Eltringham and John Readhead, all at South Shields, launched many tugs, gaining a worldwide reputation for their skills. Also of note was the business of Hepple & Co., which was at first based in the area later occupied by the Wallsend Dry Docks, and then moved to North Shields. Afterwards Hepple established its final base at South Shields where this renowned tug builder flourished for many years.

The early tugs had wooden hulls and were driven by paddles, but wood eventually gave way to iron, a material noted for its long life, and screw propulsion was also adopted in many vessels. However, paddle tugs continued in use on the Tyne well into the 20th century.

Paddle tugs were also employed as the first steam trawlers to be based on the river. Indeed, it can be said that they began the steam trawling era at the fishing port of North Shields. The man behind this development was William Purdy, of North Shields, who fitted out his tug the *Messenger* as a trawler and ventured out from the Tyne on his first trip in 1877 with two fishermen.

Purdy achieved a good catch and picked up some additional work on the way home by towing a sailing vessel into the Tyne. His success with the *Messenger* led other tug owners to use their paddle vessels for trawling. In later years, many purpose-built trawlers were to be launched on the river from yards such as those of Edwards Brothers at North Shields, which was to merge with Smith's Dock, and Eltringham at South Shields.

A considerable number of tug firms operated on the river during the 19th and 20th centuries. The Tyne was a busy port and they were needed. They included Lawson, Batey, France

The paddle tug Washington, off the Broad Landing, South Shields, 1910. She was another tug in Mauretania's escort of 1907.

Fenwick Tyne & Wear, John Dry, Ridley, Crosthwaite, Anchor, Brown, and Robert Redhead. However, after the Second World War various amalgamations meant that only two concerns dominated the tug business on the Tyne, Lawson-Batey and France Fenwick Tyne & Wear.

The separate companies of Lawson (also known as Black Diamond Tugs because of the diamond emblem on its vessels' funnels) and Batey (its funnels featured a blue Maltese cross) amalgamated in 1920 to form Lawson-Batey Steam Tugs.

France Fenwick Tyne & Wear, which had been based first on the Wear, moved into the Tyne in 1920 when it acquired the Anchor Steam Tug Company of North Shields. France Fenwick adopted the anchor emblem of this firm for its funnels.

But it was the boats rather than the companies which attracted people's attention. The iron-hulled paddle tugs seem to have been a favourite of many river watchers. These sturdy little vessels often had long lives. Two of the best examples were *President* and *Washington*. Both these hardworking craft helped to escort the famous Tyne passenger liner *Mauretania* down the Tyne for her delivery voyage to Liverpool in October 1907.

President, completed in 1876, was launched at John Readhead's yard at South Shields. She operated on the Tyne and the Wear for an extraordinary 69 years, from 1891 to 1959.

Washington was also launched at South Shields by John Readhead, during his partnership with John Softley, and was completed in 1870. This boat worked on the river from 1883 to 1952.

Also long-lived was the paddle tug *Comet*. She had been completed in 1876 and worked on the Tyne from 1897 to 1952.

Another paddle-driven vessel which put in stirling service on the river was the *Conqueror*. She had been launched by the Hepple company when it had a yard at North Shields, being completed in 1884.

Dick Keys remembers seeing the *Conqueror* on the river

The Conqueror, at Newcastle Quayside, 26 October 1946. She began her career in 1884 and was not broken up until 1956.

when he was a boy. He writes: 'During the 1940s and indeed for some years after, there were still a number of paddle tugs working on the Tyne. The one which I remember most of all was the *Conqueror*. She was a real old timer, built of iron. Black hulled with white painted paddle boxes and bright varnished woodwork, she had two tall funnels placed abreast of one another, each painted in the attractive colour scheme of her owners.

'I once watched the *Conqueror* manoeuvring off

Newcastle Quay. The loud thump of her paddles as they slapped the water, and the long swathe of white, agitated water they created exuded an impression of immense power in a way never achieved by the screw tugs.'

Ian Wilson was born and brought up in South Shields and remembers seeing some of the paddle tugs in action when he was a boy in the 1950s. His father was an engineering officer in the Merchant Navy. Ian and his friends would visit the riverside at the Mill Dam where there was always plenty of shipping to watch. The headquarters of the river police was situated there and he recalls the chief constable with golden insignia on the peak of his cap.

He writes: 'It was a place of adventure where we would go to watch the busy traffic on the river – cargo ships coming and going, tugs bustling around them and the South Shields ferry making its sedate way across the river to North Shields in a cloud of smoke from its tall funnel.

'It was the Mill Dam at South Shields, a great attraction for boys of 13 or 14 in the 1950s. I loved it, which was probably only natural as I came from a seafaring family, my dad being a marine engineer. Of course my pals and I were not supposed to go there, it was dangerous and dirty, and no doubt we would have been in trouble if our parents ever found out. But nothing could keep us away. We had lots of questions in our heads: where had the ships been to and where were they going?

'A 25-minute cycle ride and we were there, ready for adventure. And it was dirty and noisy, which made it all the more exciting. Harton Staiths was next door to the Mill Dam and colliers were constantly loading coal before setting off for the power stations of London. And what a racket, with coal dust everywhere.

'But the tugs somehow seemed to be the main attraction in spite of vessels like the Christian Salvesen whale factory ships in dry dock at the Middle Docks or lying off these docks waiting for their annual refit. The tugs were usually moored off the Mill Dam waiting for work. And there were a lot of them.'

France Fenwick's paddle tugs frequently drew Ian's attention: 'They held a special attraction because when separately driven the paddles could exert a tremendous turning force, and for this reason they were preferred under certain conditions … We enjoyed watching them bustling around guiding ships in their care down river or up river to one of the shiprepair yards. And quite often the foyboatmen would hitch a lift too.'

Among the paddle tugs he remembers were the *Eppleton Hall*, *Houghton* and *Roker*. These vessels were also frequently seen working on the Wear as well as the Tyne.

By the 1950s the paddle vessels were in a minority. Ian recalls that some of the screw-driven boats were diesel-powered but most still had steam reciprocating engines. 'Even as youngsters we realised that tug design was specialised. The hull was very strong and surrounded by a massive fender to take hard knocks. The towing hook was attached to a reinforced bulkhead amidships and placed as low as possible which made the towing rails necessary over the after deck to stop the rope fouling obstructions on deck. And the centre of gravity was low to prevent the vessel overturning. The machinery was powerful too.'

As well as the paddle boats, Ian saw numerous screw-driven tugs ranging from the old boats *Robert Redhead* and *Cullercoats* to more recent craft such as the *Alnwick* and *Impetus*.

Conqueror in Shields Harbour around 1946. She has recently been repainted to remove her wartime coat of grey. Also in the photograph are a dredger, left, a motor coaster, and the RNVR training hulk, Satellite.

The work of the river's tugs was varied and could include some interesting tows. For example, in 1913 the John Dry tug *Great Emperor*, was called upon to take a sliding gate or caisson from Swan Hunter & Wigham Richardson's Wallsend Shipyard on the Tyne to an Admiralty dry dock at Portsmouth. The caisson, which was 100ft wide, had been launched on the Wear, but was made ready for its voyage at Wallsend. *Great Emperor* was a screw-driven vessel.

The Tyne's tugs were also often in action towing newly-built vessels from the river's shipyards to sea. Sometimes the new ships were on their way to their trials and sometimes they were bound for delivery to their owners. On other occasions, major passenger liners were brought into the river. For example, in the early 1920s the Cunard liners *Mauretania*, *Aquitania* and *Berengaria* were all guided up river by flotillas of tugs for refits and to be converted from coal to oil burning. The *Aquitania* received her refit and conversion in 1919-20 at Armstrong Whitworth's Walker Naval Yard, Newcastle.

The *Mauretania* entered the Tyne in 1921. After her conversion at Swan Hunter & Wigham Richardson's Wallsend Yard, where the famed liner had been built, she left the river

Shipbuilding and Shipping Record

Berengaria is towed out to sea by the paddle tug Washington and screw tugs George V and Great Emperor on 26 April 1922.

in March 1922, being towed down the Tyne stern first by the four tugs *Joseph Crosthwaite*, *Ben Ledi*, *Great Emperor* and *Plover*. However, the great ship was turned around off Tyne Dock, so that her bows faced seawards.

The following month the *Berengaria*, an even larger liner than the *Mauretania*, was also towed down river stern first. She had undergone her oil burning conversion, like the *Aquitania*, at the Walker Naval Yard. This time eight tugs were drafted in to handle the mighty ship. They were the

Great Emperor, Francis Batey, and a sailing ship off the pilot jetty, South Shields. Foyboats are tied up in the foreground. The foyboatmen moored ships coming into the river and cast them off on their departure. The sailing ship is probably the Danish-owned Vera which took coal from the Tyne to Copenhagen in 1933.

George V, Plover, Joseph Crosthwaite, Great Emperor, Washington, Conqueror, President and *Ben Ledi*. The *Berengaria* was turned off Tyne Dock with less than 50ft of water to spare each side of the river. She reached the waters of the North Sea two hours after leaving the yard.

Ironically, the *Berengaria* was to return to the Tyne in 1938 – this time for work to start on breaking her up at Jarrow. The *Olympic*, sister ship of the ill-fated *Titanic*, had been brought to Jarrow in 1935, also for dismantling. The passage of these giant vessels up river again provided important work for the Tyne's energetic tugs. The breaking up jobs were carried out by Jarrow men who had lost their jobs when Palmers shipyard closed.

Among the numerous tugs on the river in the 20th century was Lawson-Batey's *Joffre*, named after the French army commander-in-chief during the First World War. She was a large and powerful screw-driven vessel which had been completed in 1916.

In 1924 the *Joffre* helped tow the battlecruiser HMS *Lion*, which had fought at the Battle of Jutland, from Rosyth to Jarrow for work to begin on breaking her up. She was joined in this task by the tugs *Plover*, *Francis Batey* and *Comet*.

The *Lion*, which had narrowly escaped being sunk at Jutland, was moored at Jarrow Slake for the breaking up to start. She was to remain at Jarrow for around six months. After this period had elapsed a great deal of dismantling had been carried out, but it was estimated there was still 10,000 tons of material left in the hull. In November, Redhead tugs towed her to the Palmers Hebburn Dry Dock. It then took five days for workmen to cut what was left of the ship into two sections using oxy-acetylene burners.

It was planned that one section would be towed upriver

From a River Tyne Official Handbook, 1934.

to Derwenthaugh, Dunston, and the other to Blyth where the work of dismantling would be completed. But it was found the water was too shallow at Derwenthaugh and instead both sections were taken to Blyth – another job for five of the river's tugs. They accomplished the task in two trips during which tow lines snapped more than once.

The *Lion* had visited the Tyne once before. This was during the First World War when she was taken to the Admiralty Floating Dock at Jarrow Slake to undergo repairs for damage received during the Battle of Heligoland Bight. This large dock had been built by Swan Hunter & Wigham Richardson.

In January 1953 the Norwegian ferry *Blenheim*, outward bound from the Tyne Commission Quay for Oslo, hit the *Joffre* as she lay moored at South Shields. The accident took place in thick fog. The *Joffre* received damage and her mooring lines were carried away. Luckily, no-one was hurt. She was then taken in tow by the Ridley paddle tug *Reliant*. The *Reliant* had been completed at Eltringham's yard, South Shields, in 1907 as the *Old Trafford*.

The tug crews were a hardy breed of men and their job was often hazardous. For example, in December 1946 the *Francis Batey* was towing the cargo ship *Regent Tiger*, of

Newcastle Chronicle & Journal Ltd.

The crew of the tug Joffre enjoy a break from their work in 1948.

London, from Bill Quay on the Tyne. The *Francis Batey* was positioned ahead and another tug, the *Tynesider*, astern. Within a few seconds the *Francis Batey* heeled over on to her side. It was not long before she sank.

Men working at R.B. Harrison's shiprepair yard at Bill Quay then saw the tug's six crewmen struggling in the water. Also at the yard were men from the tug *Washington* which was undergoing repairs there. Men from both groups climbed into small boats and managed to rescue the *Francis Batey*'s crew, all of whom were from South Shields.

An engine room man had a particularly narrow escape. Water poured through the port skylight and also down the ladders, threatening to drown him. Fortunately, the mate helped him up through the skylight. Moments later they were in the river and soon they were picked up by the boats. The engine room crewman later recalled that if he had not been rescued he would never had reached the shore by himself.

Once safely landed at the yard, the crew of the *Washington* provided the *Francis Batey*'s men with dry clothing. The Lawson-Batey tug *Homer* was then called to the scene and took the rescued crew to the ferry landing at South Shields. Cars were waiting there to take them to their homes after their ordeal in the cold waters of the river.

The Tyne Improvement Commission declared the wreck of the tug a danger to navigation and the spot was marked and lighted by *No 2 Wreck Boat*. However, the following month the *Francis Batey* was raised and taken to Smith's Dock at North Shields for repairs. The tug had been built on the opposite bank of the river, at South Shields, by Hepple & Co, being completed in 1914. The *Francis Batey* also served for a while at Blyth and did not go the breaker's yard until 1968. She had led a highly useful life, like her hard-working crewmen.

Shipbuilding and Shipping Record

The battle cruiser Lion enters the Tyne in March 1924 to be broken up. Plover, Joffre and Francis Batey towed the 698 ft long ship into the river to a temporary berth at Jarrow Slake.

The floating hospital

Tyneside was visited by cholera epidemics on four occasions during the 19th century. In 1871 the local authorities bordering the river began preventative measures with the creation of the Port of Tyne Sanitary Authority. The crews of all arriving ships were inspected for health problems. Any suspected cases of infectious diseases were isolated aboard a floating hospital which was moored at Jarrow Slake.

The first such hospital was the *Tyne*, a former ferry, which was fitted out with a 14-bed ward. Later she was joined by what was described as a 'disinfecting hulk' – an old ship given a new use. In 1883 a former Dutch schooner, named *Alliance*, was converted to take ten patients.

About three years later all three were replaced by a purpose-built floating hospital. It was constructed at the shipyard of Wood Skinner at Bill Quay. Launched into the Tyne in August 1886, the new floating hospital featured four wards with a total of 30 beds. The whole structure rested on ten cylindrical pontoons.

During 1886 six cases of enteric fever were admitted to the hospital. Five of the patients recovered and one died. There were also two cases of suspected enteric fever and one patient had German measles. Two of the men with fever were crew members of the sailing vessel *Susannah Thrift*. The medical officer of health reported: 'The water in this case was bad, and was ordered to be changed.'

The *Susannah Thrift*, a brigantine, had arrived from the Thames. H.Y. Moffat, in his book *From Ship's-Boy to*

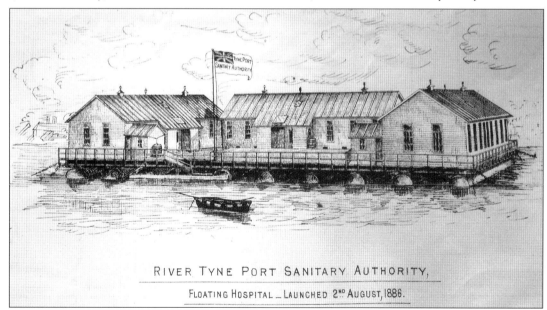

RIVER TYNE PORT SANITARY AUTHORITY,

FLOATING HOSPITAL _ LAUNCHED 2ND AUGUST, 1886.

The Floating Hospital at Jarrow Slake, 1886, from the Annual Report of the Medical Officer of Health.

Skipper, told of his experiences aboard the Tyne collier *Premium* in the 1860s. He noted that 'we always filled our water casks from the river (Thames) at half ebb, and we did the same at Hamburg, but there the river was clearer water than the Thames'. How many seamen died from water-borne diseases, such as cholera and dysentery, by drinking water from rivers will never be known. It is possible the men from the *Susannah Thrift* contracted enteric fever from the Thames. It would have been equally unwise to drink from the 'coaly' Tyne.

The port health authority was clearly proud of its new facility. In describing the wards a report declared: 'They are spacious, light and airy apartments, having large windows and special means of ventilation. The interior is lined with polished pitch pine in narrow strips.

'In each ward there is a central shaft through the roof, fitted with Kite's patent ventilator for carrying off vitiated air. Near the doors there is a series of ventilators for the admission of fresh air, and under the floor of each apartment an air-space of about ten inches, which will secure a constant circulation of fresh air.

'Between the surface of the river and the platform, a space of four feet, there will be a perfectly free current of pure air. The rise and fall of the tides and the current produced by the spaces between the pontoons will prevent the possibility of any impurity existing beneath the hospital.'

The hospital was divided into several small wards, some with six and others with four beds. Between each six and four-bed ward was a nurse's apartment or office with glazed doors on either side so that the nurse could command a view of the patients. An open-air platform at the front of the hospital was said to provide ample space 'for the recreation of convalescent patients'.

In September 1886 one of the crew of the Chilean warship *Blanco Encalada*, while being treated at the Newcastle Infirmary for another condition, developed smallpox. He was removed to the Newcastle Smallpox Hospital, which was situated on the Town Moor. No other cases of the disease were reported aboard the vessel. The *Blanco Encalada* was undergoing a refit at Armstrong Mitchell's Elswick Yard, Newcastle.

Ten years after the new floating hospital at Jarrow Slake began operation its nurses and doctors were still being kept busy with seamen who had acquired various illnesses. For example, in April 1896 three of the crew of the steamer *Ashley*, a British ship which had arrived in the Tyne from South America, were admitted to the hospital with typhoid fever. The *Ashley* was disinfected and fresh water was ordered for drinking and cooking aboard. The ship was a Tyne-built one, having been completed by Palmers of Jarrow in 1876.

A few days later another seaman was brought to the hospital. He was a fireman aboard the steamer *Stelling*, which had arrived from Boulogne in France, and who was suffering from an extremely sore throat and 'suspicious rash'. He was diagnosed as having scarlet fever.

By the end of April a new patient had been admitted. He was a crewman from the newly-built Russian Volunteer Fleet steamer *Kerson*, which was preparing to leaving the Tyne after being completed at Hawthorn Leslie's Hebburn shipyard. This man was said to be suffering from a 'venereal complaint'.

In early May, the sailing ship *Forthbank* entered the river from Santos via Port Adelaide. Nineteen of the crew were reported as having suffered from yellow fever on the voyage and eight of these had died at sea. The vessel had been disinfected at Port Adelaide. On arrival in the Tyne all the remaining crew members were found to be well. However, the Port of Tyne Sanitary Authority was taking no chances – the crew accommodation area was disinfected.

The Tyne Steam Shipping Company, which ran steamers to Rotterdam, Hamburg, Antwerp and Ghent as well as London, was well aware of the potential health dangers aboard ships and of the risk of bringing diseases into the river.

In 1892, the company's secretary and manager, Richard Welford, issued the following strict instructions to captains: 'In view of the outbreak of cholera abroad, please note the following regulations. If any person dies on board of cholera or suspected cholera, the body must be buried at sea at least six miles from land, with sufficient weight to sink it, and a proper entry of the fact must be made in the official log, signed by all the officers of the ship, and any other independent witness that can be obtained, such witnesses to sign their full names and addresses.

'If the vessel comes into port with a dead body on board it will be ordered out to sea to perform the operation of burial. The same thing will occur if any person dies coming up the river, and in such case a vessel will have to go into quarantine for 24 hours in order that she may be sufficiently disinfected.'

In 1909, the floating hospital must have been overcrowded. No less than 40 crewmen from the Brazilian cruiser *Barroso*, which was paying a visit to the Tyne, were admitted to its wards with beri-beri, a disease caused by a vitamin deficiency. One man died, but it seems that all the others

PRECAUTIONS
AGAINST
CHOLERA.

Several Cases of Asiatic Cholera have occurred in Seaport Towns upon the Continent, and there is reason to fear that, unless great precautions are taken, the disease may extend to this Country.

Under these circumstances all Persons employed on board the Tyne Steam Shipping Company's Steamers are earnestly advised to refrain from entering low Public Houses abroad; to avoid eating unwholesome Meat and Vegetables, and indigestible food generally; to preserve the utmost cleanliness consistent with their occupation, making free use of cold water; to see that their Mattresses and Bedding are well aired every day; and, above all things, to avoid excesses of every kind when ashore.

BY ORDER.

Newcastle-upon-Tyne : Printed by M. BENSON, 61, Side—opposite the Foot of Dean Street.

In 1892 the Tyne Steam Shipping Co. warned its staff about the dangers of infection.

recovered. The *Barroso* had been launched at the Elswick Shipyard, Newcastle, in 1896.

The floating hospital was a feature of the river at Jarrow Slake for nearly 45 years. It was not broken up until 1930 and is believed to have been the last of its type in the world.

Loading coals on the Tyne, 1901. A spout or chute protrudes from the end of the staith and a coal truck can be seen above. The ship being loaded is the Raphael.

Coals to Newcastle

Of all the many ships entering and departing from the Tyne, colliers were by far the most numerous and familiar. The carrying of coals from the river dated back centuries.

Sailing vessels totally dominated the coal trade up until the early 1850s, but because they were dependent on the vagaries of the wind they lacked the speed and regularity of the new steamships which began to appear on the scene. The most famous of the early steam colliers was the iron-hulled, propeller-driven *John Bowes*, launched by Palmers of Jarrow in 1852. She demonstrated conclusively the advantages of using steam power and from then on the sailing colliers went into gradual decline.

NEW LINE OF SCREW STEAMERS BETWEEN NEWCASTLE AND LONDON.

THE Shippers and Receivers of Goods are respectfully informed that Messrs. PALMER BROTHERS and Co. (at the earnest Solicitation of a Number of Manufacturers and others,) have consented to place the large First-class New Iron Screw Steam-ship JOHN BOWES (600 Tons Burthen,) on this Station and Arrangements have been made for her to Sail from NEWCASTLE, on *Saturday, March 5, 1853*, at Ten Morning, returning from LONDON on *Friday the 11th current*, and thereafter to Sail from each End every alternate Friday, until a Consort Steamer is ready in April, when a Weekly Communication will be Established.

Freights moderate.—Apply to
WM. LAING, Jun. & Co.
General Shipping Agency Office,
New Quay, Newcastle, 23rd February, 1853.

A steamer, probably on her way to load coal at Dunston Staiths, approaches the open Swing Bridge around 1900.

The introduction of steam colliers in the 19th century helped to generate a great increase in shipments of 'black diamonds' from the Tyne. One of the most important markets was the gas industry of London which needed a plentiful and regular supply of coal to produce gas lighting for the capital's streets. In the 20th century the power stations of the electricity industry would also provide vital work for the colliers.

A large number of the crewmen aboard these little steamers were from the North-East, particularly the Tyneside area. It was a dusty, dirty job, and during the the two world wars a dangerous one. U-boats and mines were a constant danger on the East Coast route to the Thames during the First World War, and in the Second World War the crews faced the peril of E-boats. These were fast German motor boats which carried guns and torpedoes and were capable of laying mines. Many collier men lost their lives as the result of enemy action.

Among the most prominent of the companies operating colliers along the East Coast was Stephenson Clarke. By 1937 it was managing an entire fleet of these ships for the Gas Light and Coke Company and also for the large electricity concerns of the London Power Company, Fulham Borough Council and Brighton Corporation.

Deliveries to works far up the Thames, such as those at Battersea, Fulham and Wandsworth, were made by specially designed colliers known as 'flat-irons' or 'flatties'. These up-river ships had very low superstructures with hinged funnels and hinged or telescopic masts, which could be lowered, enabling them to pass under the numerous Thames bridges.

South Tyneside MBC

Storm damage to the North Pier in 1897.

The first flat-irons had appeared as early as 1878, when Palmers Shipyard at Jarrow completed the *Westminster* and *Vauxhall*, designed to deliver coal from the North-East to the Nine Elms Gas Works at Vauxhall, London.

Before 1850, which was the era of sailing colliers, coal exports from the Tyne had grown to about five and quarter million tons a year, but between then and the early 1900s the shipments increased enormously. In 1911 more than 20 millions tons of coal and coke was exported from the river to London, the South-East and other ports throughout the world. In 1913 exports again reached over 20 million tons. Although this figure fell during the First World War, shipments recovered afterwards, reaching more than 21 million tons in 1923.

This booming seaborne trade was greatly assisted in 1850 by the establishment of the Tyne Improvement Commission which made the river one of the best ports on the East Coast. Beginning in the 1860s, the commission carried out major dredging operations which deepened the Tyne and enabled it to take larger ships as well as improving life for the smaller ones. Up to the end of 1933 more than 160 million tons of material had been dredged from the Tyne and taken away to sea.

The treacherous bar at the mouth of the river was gradually dredged away and the Tyne, for a distance of 14 miles inland from the mouth, was widened and straightened. In addition, two magnificent protective piers were constructed at the river's entrance, an achievement which still impresses visitors today.

Work began on the North Pier in 1854 but was beset with problems, the pier being breached by storms in 1867, and again, more seriously, in 1897. The structure was therefore redesigned to make it straight rather than curved. The North Pier was finally completed in 1909

and opened to the public the following year.

The longer South Pier was begun in the same year as the North, but was also breached by the storm of 1867. In 1894 the structure received further storm damage. Despite this setback, the South Pier was completed in 1895.

Like two great protective arms, these piers made the Tyne one of the most important harbours of refuge on the East Coast for vessels sheltering from storms or in distress.

The commission also improved facilities for the loading of coal so that steamers could take on their cargoes quickly

Loading coal on the Tyne, around 1897. Trimmers with their heart-shaped shovels wait on the right. Coal cascaded down the chute from the staith into the hold.

and efficiently. The Tyne gained a well deserved reputation as a port for bunkering as well as loading of coal cargoes. Ships seeking coal to refuel their engines could speedily and cheaply replenish their bunkers at staiths (loading jetties or platforms, generally timber-built) not far from the river mouth and so achieve a quick turn-around time at low cost.

Ships were attended to at the staiths by shore-based workmen known as teemers and trimmers. The teemers carried out the actual loading of vessels, operating the equipment needed for this process. The trimmers, armed with shovels, would level out the coal in the holds, helping to ensure stability and enabling the hatches to be closed by 'knocking the top off' the black diamonds.

By 1925 there were six major coal-loading points on the Tyne, all linked by railways to the pits. They were: Tyne Dock, Dunston Staiths, and West Dunston Staiths, owned by the London and North Eastern Railway (formerly the North Eastern Railway); Northumberland Dock and Whitehill Point Staiths, owned by the Tyne Improvement Commission; and Derwenthaugh Staiths, owned by the Consett Iron Company. All were equipped with gravity loading spouts (also known as chutes) and electric conveyor belts. Staiths were also provided by the Tyne Improvement Commission at the Albert Edward Dock, North Shields.

In addition there was a considerable number of smaller staiths, generally owned by colliery companies, including Harton Staiths at South Shields, and those at Wallsend, Hebburn, Felling, Elswick, Jarrow (Springwell), Heworth, Scotswood, Lemington, Blaydon and Stella.

The Harton Coal Company advertises in the River Tyne Official Handbook, 1934.

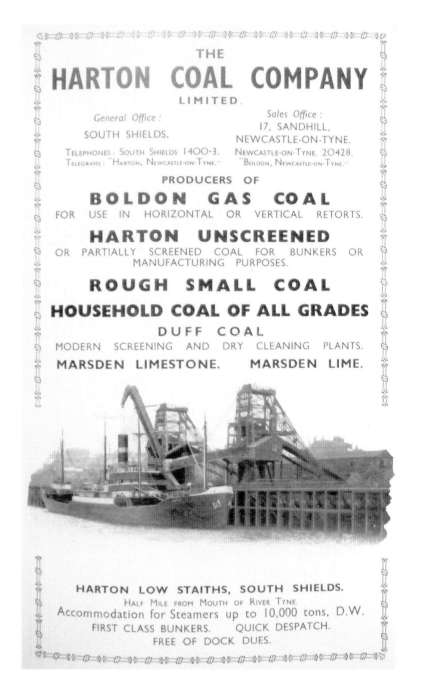

South Tyneside MBC

Harton Staiths, South Shields, where coal from the Harton Coal Company's pits was loaded.

One of the most important facilities was Tyne Dock, opened in 1859 on the south bank, which by 1925 had exported more coal than any other dock in the world. In 1908, 7.5 million tons of coal and coke had gushed from its staiths into the holds of waiting ships. A figure of over 7 millions tons was again achieved in 1913. The dock featured four staiths which enabled 16 vessels to load at the same time. Two or more spouts could be operated on one steamer simultaneously, so rapid loading was possible. There were 42 spouts and eight electric conveyor belts.

If required, Tyne Dock, as well as Dunston and Derwenthaugh staiths, could operate continuous loading day and night, although the more usual weekday loading hours at most of the river's staiths were from 6am to 10pm. Overtime was sometimes worked up to midnight. On Saturdays, the hours were 6am to 12 noon and this could be extended to 10pm if needed.

At Northumberland Dock, Howdon, which was opened in 1857 on the north side of the river, there were eight staiths, four operated by coal companies of South East Northumberland and four by the London and North Eastern Railway.

Also on the north side, on a bend in the river immediately to the east of Northumberland Dock, were the Whitehill Point Staiths. These were often used by bunkering ships which did not have time to enter the dock and which could be replenished with coal at any state of the tide. However, the staiths also loaded colliers with their cargo. The facility featured three hydraulic lifts which could raise trucks up to 45ft above the jetties, allowing large ships to be coaled by electric conveyor belts no matter how high the tide.

Ten miles up river, beyond the great bridges across the Tyne between Newcastle and Gateshead, lay the important Dunston Staiths, opened in 1893. These were built to handle the output of coal from pits west of central Newcastle and Gateshead to save the time and cost involved in the rail journey to docks nearer the river mouth. A second set of staiths was added to the facility in 1903.

At Dunston, the loading of ships could also be undertaken at any state of the tide, a tribute to the dredging work of the Tyne Improvement Commission. Each berth had two gravity spouts and there were three electric conveyor belts.

Colliers would steam up river to Dunston, moving through the Swing Bridge which had opened for them. Crowds of walkers on the Newcastle and Gateshead side would wait patiently for them to pass.

As a ship approached the bridge, from either direction, she sounded three blasts on her steam whistle. The Swing Bridge then answered this signal with three blasts from its own siren and the opening machinery was started. The year 1924 saw 6,007 vessels pass through the bridge, the majority of them colliers. When near to Dunston Staiths the colliers would generally moor at lines of buoys, known as tiers, joining a queue of vessels waiting for their turn to load. Most of these staiths, which closed in 1980, still survive today, despite a section being destroyed by fire in recent years. Their extensive timber structure constitutes a monument to the once booming coal trade.

About a mile further up river were the West Dunston Staiths, opened in 1923, expanding the facilities to meet increased demand. Further up river still were the Derwenthaugh Staiths. These were a little to the east of the Scotswood Bridge and close to the mouth of the Derwent, a tributary of the Tyne.

In the 1930s two new staiths were opened at Howdon and Jarrow, featuring electric conveyor belts which delivered the coal to special towers from which it was loaded into the waiting ships. The Howdon Staith, at the western end of Northumberland Dock, was opened in December 1932.

Coal, won from the earth by the North-East's courageous miners, flowed out from the river aboard the colliers in seemingly endless measure, fuelling steam locomotives, ships and providing homes, factories, offices, and hospitals with their heating and lighting. In material terms, it was perhaps the North-East's greatest contribution to civilisation.

However, in 1926 the great flood of black diamonds from the 'coaly' Tyne was reversed. A case of 'carrying coals to Newcastle' occurred during the miners' strike of that year which culminated in the General Strike.

A picture postcard features Dunston Staiths around 1900. They still survive in spite of fire damage in recent years.

The import of coal into the Tyne began in June 1926, a month after the miners' strike began. It was reported that by mid-July eight cargoes totalling around 8,000 tons had arrived in the river. Ships from Germany and the United States delivered the largest amounts. It did not come cheap and the main buyers were the Newcastle & Gateshead Gas Company and the London and North Eastern Railway.

During the strike, the North Shields fishing trawler fleet was said to have operated on 50 per cent of their normal bunker supplies and it was later reported that the largest trawlers were laid up because of the high price of imported coal.

By the end of the miners' strike in November 1926 over 262,000 tons of coal had been brought into the Tyne from the USA, 118,000 tons from Germany, 25,000 tons from Holland, and smaller amounts from countries including Belgium, France, Spain and Sweden.

Even when the strike ended, foreign coal continued to be brought into the river for a while in order to fulfil contracts.

The wreck of the Richard Welford as pictured in Shipbuilding and Shipping Record on 9 August 1923.

Capsizings, collisions and cranes

The Newcastle and Gateshead quaysides were the scene of several dramatic incidents during the days when they were busy with shipping. On 2 August 1923 the Tyne-Tees Steam Shipping Company's vessel *Richard Welford*, named after the firm's secretary, arrived at Newcastle Quay from Rotterdam. She was carrying two passengers and a cargo of 800 tons of potatoes.

The passengers disembarked and gangs of dockers began unloading the potatoes through side doors onto the quay. An hour or so later the ship began to list. Indeed, the *Richard Welford* leaned over so much that water began pouring in over the lower lip of the side doors.

The situation became so dangerous that the ship's master, Captain A. Lawrence, gave orders that everyone on board should leave the vessel. A stewardess, a Miss Stevens, who had been sleeping in her bunk as the water level rose, was rescued by a steward. He carried her on deck, still in her nightdress, and handed her to two men on the quay. All of Miss Stevens' belongings were lost as the ship capsized. However, one crew member was missing. He was Ralph Hewitt, from Wallsend, a fireman. Tragically, the unfortunate man was drowned in his bunk.

The *Richard Welford*'s mast hit the quay and snapped off as the ship toppled over. Her funnel fell into the river. The ship then sank on her side, her hull still visible at low tide. It was to be over two months before she was raised and taken to Smith's Dock at North Shields for extensive repairs.

The *Richard Welford* had previously been employed on the Newcastle-London service, but had been replaced by the newly-built *Bernicia* and *Hadrian*.

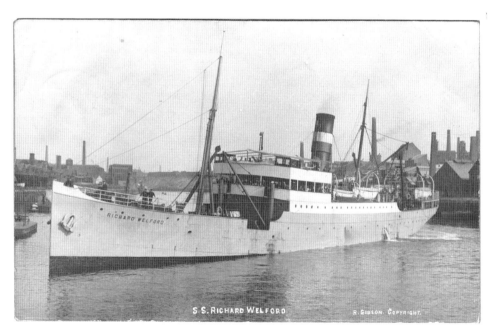

The Richard Welford, from a postcard mailed in 1908.

Another dramatic incident occurred in June 1929, but fortunately did not involve loss of life. About 80ft of the quay wall at the Tyne-Tees Steam Shipping Company's Gateshead wharf collapsed into the river. The wharf was used by steamers on some of the firm's continental routes. Others, and those on the London service, berthed on the Newcastle side.

More than a year later, in September 1930, a further portion of the quay at the Gateshead wharf collapsed. This time, about 150 tons of masonry ended up in the river and there was little left of the original quay. Work had already begun on reconstruction of the first section to collapse. Luckily, no-one was hurt in the second incident as the quay had shown signs that it was about to give way. It was all eventually rebuilt.

Jimmy Forsyth

Local photographer Jimmy Forsyth captured the salvaged Cyprian Coast lying off Newcastle Quayside between flotation tanks in January 1956.

Another drama unfolded in December 1955 when the motor vessel *Cyprian Coast*, formerly the Tyne-Tees Steam Shipping Company's *Alnwick*, sank off Newcastle Quay after a collision involving a Swedish ship, the *Arabert*. The *Cyprian Coast* had been turning towards Gateshead Quay to berth when the collision occurred. The *Arabert* was on her way to sea with an escort of tugs.

Following the impact, some of the crew of the *Cyprian Coast* were rescued from the water by men from the *Arabert*; one man jumped into a tug, and two others managed to reach a dinghy. In less than ten minutes the ship had sunk into the river, with part of her bow protruding above the water. Her stern settled so that it touched the river bed.

The ship was now clearly a danger to navigation. Accordingly, a powerful tug was drafted in to pull the wreck of the *Cyprian Coast* away from the centre of the north shipping channel towards Newcastle Quay. Early the next year, the vessel was raised and towed to Clelland's Slipway at Willington Quay by the tugs *Homer* and *Northsider*. She eventually returned to service.

Other reaches of the Tyne have also seen numerous accidents. Perhaps the most unusual was that involving the first *Titan* floating crane. The German-built *Titan* was ordered by shipbuilders Swan Hunter & Wigham Richardson to help with the *Mauretania* contract, arriving on the river in 1906. She lifted the huge turbines and boilers into the *Mauretania* during the fitting-out of the great passenger liner at the Wallsend Shipyard.

This heavy-lift floating crane was wrecked in December 1921 when a westerly gale caused her to break loose from her moorings at Hebburn and she was swept down river, colliding with several vessels. The wreck of the *Titan* was eventually towed out into the North Sea and sunk.

The accident happened in the early morning darkness of Christmas Eve 1921. The crane had been moored close to the Hawthorn Leslie shipyard when she broke away as the wind raged along the river. The *Titan* at first collided with the moored tug *Cambrian*, owned by the workless shipyard of Renwick and Dalgleish between Hebburn and Jarrow. The tug was sunk.

The crane was then swept further down river to Jarrow where she hit the steamer *Cairnside*, of Sunderland, which was lying moored at No 1 tier, Jarrow. This caused the *Cairnside* also to break adrift and disturb the moorings of two other ships, the steamers *Benwood*, of Liverpool, and

The Titan I crane towers over a Brazilian battleship at the Elswick shipyard around 1913.

Arthur Von Gwinner, of London, lying at No 2 tier. These vessels then drifted alongside Palmers Jetty at Jarrow. The crane also hit the steamer *Horden* which was lying at Jarrow staiths. A hole was punched in the side of the *Horden*.

The *Titan* continued to be driven down river by the gale, clipping the ex-German minelayer *Eskimo* and the steamer *Firwood*, lying at the tier off the Jarrow Cement Works. The crane then heeled over and sank near Purdy's Coal Hulk at the Northumberland Dock river buoys. The wreck of the *Titan* and the tug *Cambrian* were declared dangers to navigation.

Mystery surrounded the whereabouts of a watchman who was believed to have been aboard the crane when she broke loose. Several people heard the *Titan's* horn sounding in the darkness. The fate of this man does not appear to have been reported at the time.

The Dutch-built *Titan II* floating crane, capable of lifting up to 150 imperial tons, was bought by Swan Hunter & Wigham Richardson as a replacement for the ill-fated first. She made her appearance in the Tyne in 1922. Swan's formed a company with Wallsend Slipway & Engineering and Hawthorn Leslie to operate the crane and hire it out for work up and down the river.

This second crane was fitted to a new barge in c.1979 and renamed *Titan III*. The name is perhaps a little misleading since there have been three barges but only two cranes. *Titan III* is still based at the Wallsend Shipyard.

Titan III is certainly a heavy lifter, but the most powerful crane on the Tyne is the famous hammerhead (cantilever) one which was installed at the Walker Naval Yard, Newcastle, between the First and Second World Wars.

This fixed-position crane, which still dominates the river-

The Titan II floating crane lifts a gate for a new dry dock at Swan Hunter and Wigham Richardson, Wallsend, 1934.

side at Walker, has a lifting capacity of up to 250 imperial tons. Shipbuilding men nicknamed it *Goliath* and this metal giant was particularly useful for lifting heavy guns and turrets aboard large warships and for other jobs requiring great strength during the fitting out of vessels.

A much smaller crane was fitted on top of the hammerhead crane's gib. This was for lifting light weights when use of the main machinery would have been uneconomic. *Goliath* carries on his back a 'little brother'.

Goliath narrowly missed being hit by a German bomb during the Second World War. However, the crane was still standing at the end of hostilities in 1945. The mighty lifter, now painted yellow, is still used, although the Walker Naval Yard has gone.

The magnificent *Goliath* and *Titan* are sturdy survivors of a river which has seen many changes. They remain impressive examples of the crane builder's art.

The hammerhead crane, left, nick-named Goliath, towers above Walker Offshore Technology Park, c.1990. This was the site of the former Walker Naval Yard.

The river was a fascinating place for children with countless ships to watch and cranes to admire. This photograph dates from around 1950.

The Geordie tramp steamers

In the 20th century the backbone of the Tyne's shipowning industry was its fleet of 'tramps'. Unlike the cargo and passenger 'liners' which were vessels running to an advertised schedule and working on a regular trade between particular ports, the tramps carried cargoes to, or from, any destination as required. For just over 100 years, the Geordie tramp ship, steam or motor-driven, could be found at almost any port in the world where she was needed.

Joseph Robinson & Sons, Walter Runciman & Co., Hall Brothers, R. Chapman & Sons, Stephens, Sutton Ltd., R.S. Dalgliesh, W.A. Souter & Co. and B.J. Sutherland & Co., are just a few of the many tramp ship owners, or managers, which survived well into the second half of the 20th century. These concerns bore the names of their founders. They generally functioned as management companies of other shipping companies or 'lines' as they were often called – more often than not created by the managers themselves.

Robinson's Stag Line, Runciman's Moor Line, Stephens, Sutton's Red R Steamship Company and Dalgliesh's Watergate Steamship Company are typical examples. The managers usually provided the directors and owned a substantial shareholding in these companies, but this was not always the case, particularly during both world wars when they were called upon to manage ships for the government. The founders of these businesses were hard-working, resilient men operating in an intensely competitive environment.

Port of Tyne Official Handbook, 1957

THE LONGEST ESTABLISHED SHIPOWNERS IN THE NORTH OF ENGLAND

STAG LINE, LIMITED

JOSEPH ROBINSON & SONS,
MANAGERS

FOUNDED 1846

Dry cargo Tramp Fleet.

S.S. GARDENIA	6485 TONS DW.	S.S. CLINTONIA	10170 TONS DW.
M.V. CAMELLIA	7800 TONS DW.	M.V. NEWBUILDING	10200 TONS DW.
S.S. CYDONIA	8180 TONS DW.	S.S. ZINNIA	10550 TONS DW.

**I, HOWARD STREET,
NORTH SHIELDS.**

Telegrams : ROBINSON, NORTH SHIELDS.   Telephone : NORTH SHIELDS 7.

Among these luminaries of the Tyne shipping scene was Joseph Robinson. His father, James, a ship master, had accumulated enough money by 1817 to buy a small brig, *The Blessing*. She was to become the foundation stone of a tramp ship owning dynasty which was to survive for 166 years. It was the longest lived tramp outfit of them all. Maritime Chambers, the distinctive building at the foot of Howard Street, North Shields, which housed the offices of Robinson's Stag Line for 90 years, still stands, high above Shields Harbour. The exterior of the building bears the company's stag emblem.

Like the Robinson's, many of the early tramp owners had been sailing ship men. Daniel Stephens, of Stephens, Sutton Ltd., first sailed on the waters of the Tyne as an eight-year-old aboard his father's schooner *King of Tyre* when she entered the river in 1847 laden with a cargo of currants from the island of Zante.

Daniel Stephens went on to command clipper-schooners in the Azores fruit trade before coming to Newcastle in 1871 with his hard-earned savings considerably enlarged by a salvage award, to seek his fortune as a ship owner. He succeeded. When he died in 1926, aged 85, well over 40 tramp steamers, sailing for the Red R Steamship Co., had been managed by him over the years.

Another of the shipping personalities of the Tyne was sea captain Walter Runciman, who held commands in both sail and steam, before coming ashore in 1884 with his savings and some money earned by a small amount of trading on the side. It was enough to buy an elderly steamer. Running her as economically as he could, she made good money and when sold, five years later, fetched double what he had paid for her.

When Runciman died in 1937 he left wealth valued at more than £2.25m, a colossal sum by the standards of his day. Perhaps even more valuable were his writings which give

The tramp steamer Sandyford had a varied career. She was completed in 1904 at Sunderland for Sandyford SS Co. Ltd, Newcastle. In 1911 she was sold to London owners who renamed her Lodorer and in 1915 she was hired as a collier by the Admiralty. She was commissioned as HMS Farnborough (alias 'Q5') for use as a decoy ship ('Q' ship) and armed. She sank two U-boats.

a fascinating insight into the North-East Coast shipping industry of the period, both ashore and afloat. His book, *Before the Mast – And After* (London, 1924) is something of a maritime classic. For a number of years, leading up to the First World War, Walter Runciman controlled the largest tramp fleet owned on the river. They sailed under the name Moor Line.

The background and early business experience of the Hall Brothers, John and James, was very different to those already mentioned. The scions of an old Northumbrian family, not for them the heaving deck of a collier brig or schooner but a tall stool in the counting houses of merchants and ship owners. The pair made their first foray into ship owning with the purchase, in January 1854, of a tiny schooner called the *Fairy*. She was only just over 65ft long, but within little more than a couple of decades they were running a fleet which included 20 or so tramp steamers.

James Hall died in 1904, revered for his exertions in the fight for legislation to prevent overloaded ships putting to sea. He did the spade work and Samuel Plimsoll provided the political clout – and got most of the credit – to a movement which culminated in the adoption of the Load Line in the Merchant Shipping Act of 1876 without which many good men would have met watery graves. James Hall selflessly placed human life above profit. Indeed, he made it clear he was prepared to see foreign competitors triumph rather than allow British ships to be dangerously overloaded. He stands out as a humanitarian in what was a tough world of seaborne trade.

Shipbuilding and Shipping Record

The Linerton, owned by R. Chapman & Co., had an unfortunate maiden voyage from the Tyne in November 1919. She was on her way to Baltimore but after an engine breakdown off Flamborough Head had to be towed back to the Tyne. Matters worsened when bad weather caused the tow ropes to break and after going ashore near South Shields pier she broke in two. Both halves were refloated and towed to Rotterdam where she was reconstructed as an oil tanker. She is pictured grounded at South Shields.

Also in the galaxy of Tyne tramp owners was Ralph Chapman, who came from farming stock. By 1863, at the age of 30, he is described as a ship broker. Eight years later he was managing owner of a former China clipper, which had been reduced to hauling cargoes of coal to Southern Spain. The move to tramp steamers, within a partnership, came in 1871. It lasted until 1896 when the firm of R. Chapman & Sons was formed to take over four tramp tramp steamers previously managed by the partnership. By 1950 Chapman's, based in Newcastle, had become the largest tramp owners on the Tyne with a fleet numbering 16 vessels. Ralph Chapman had died in 1921 leaving an estate valued at more than £300,000, a considerable sum for the time.

Robert Stanley Dalgliesh had a career which literally saw him rise and fall. He was the son of a Newcastle doctor. Born in 1872, Dalgliesh began his commercial career in the offices of Henry Scholefield & Sons, tramp owners and ship brokers. In 1906, he left this business to launch his own tramp firm. In the early years he struggled along with only one or two vessels in commission at any one time. But between 1917 and 1920 no fewer than 23 steamers were acquired, although this number was much reduced in the difficult trading years that were to follow.

Dalgliesh died in March 1944 only four days after being released from prison on medical grounds. He had been convicted in July of the previous year on charges of conspiracy and bribery. This fall from grace – it was not the first in the history of Tyne ship owners – has to be set against his achievements. Along with Runciman, it was he who first introduced motor ships into the ranks of the Geordie tramps.

Dalgliesh also pioneered the Tyne's trade to Port Churchill, in the Hudson Bay, Canada, by sending the *Farnworth* there in 1931. It was a risky business but he made a profit on the voyage of over £6,000, even after paying out a hefty insurance premium. The venture developed into a liner trade, with general cargo being carried outwards and wheat grain homeward. The Dalgliesh Line was till sending ships to the Hudson Bay on regular summer voyages until 1970.

William Alfred Souter came to Newcastle from Sheffield in 1896. Nine years later he launched his own tramp owning firm – the Sheaf Steam Shipping Company with himself as manager. Four other companies were to follow. For the first

Port of Tyne Official Handbook, 1959

R. S. DALGLIESH
LIMITED

SHIPOWNERS · SHIPBROKERS

**WATERGATE BUILDINGS
NEWCASTLE UPON TYNE**

Grams : " VAPEUR "   Phone : NEWCASTLE 27161 (4 lines)
Telex No. : 53-321

DALGLIESH LINE
TYNE
TO
CHURCHILL
MANITOBA

LOADING TYNE AND/OR OTHER U.K. AND
CONTINENTAL PORTS

JULY and SEPTEMBER SAILINGS

CARGO TAKEN ON THROUGH RATES AND BILLS OF
LADING TO ALL POINTS IN CANADA, ESPECIALLY
SASKATCHEWAN, MANITOBA AND ALBERTA

50 years his ships were a mixed bunch of coastal/short sea trade colliers and ocean-going tramps. From the late 1950s a move was made into purpose-built ore and bulk dry cargo carriers. When he died, in December 1968, his company was managing nine such vessels.

In 1935 Souter's Sheaf Steam Shipping Company, based in Newcastle, was hit by tragedy when one of its ships disappeared with the loss of a crew of 20, most of them from

Port of Tyne Official Handbook, 1957

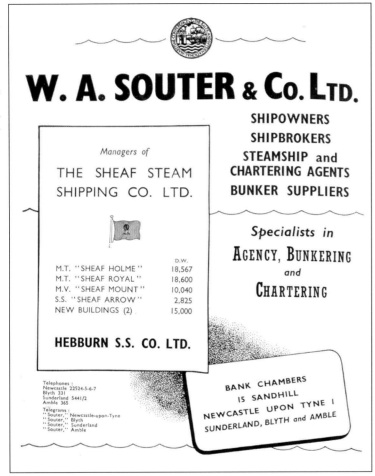

Tyneside. The ship was the *Sheaf Brook*, which on 19 November that year sailed from Springwell Staiths, Jarrow, with coal, bound for Hamburg.

The following day the *Sheaf Brook* sent out an SOS message for help when 110 miles east-south-east of the Tyne. The radio information included the message: 'Require assistance. Cabin flooded. Dangerous list to port.'

The SOS prompted a sister ship, the *Sheaf Water*, into immediate action. She steamed at full speed to the position given by the vessel in distress. When the *Sheaf Water* reached the reported position of the *Sheaf Brook* there was no ship to be seen, but she sighted an upturned lifeboat and floating wreckage. Three rockets were seen to the north-north-west.

The *Sheaf Water* continued the search in the direction of the rockets and sent out the radio message: 'Have sighted three rockets. If you hear our wireless send up more rockets.' But no more were seen.

The missing ship's master was Captain C.E. Brown, of Jesmond, Newcastle, who had a wife and one child. It was the first ship he had commanded. The mate, M. Peterson, of South Shields, had served in the *Sheaf Brook* for six months and had survived being torpedoed during the First World War. The third engineer, W. Richardson, also from South Shields, was the father of two boys.

Able Seaman William Stoten, from Tyne Dock, had only recently joined the vessel after being unemployed for eight months. He had a wife and four children. Steward R.

Shipbuilding and Shipping Record

Souter's Sheaf Field in 1923. She was mined in October 1940.

Hodgson, of South Shields, had a wife and two children. Also among those lost was mess room boy A.E. Wharrier, of Dunston.

William Souter's life saw the flow of coal and coke from the Tyne slump from a staggering 21.5 million tons in 1923 to a mere drip by the 1960s. He also saw the tramps carry essential cargoes through two world wars (he lost a son in the second) and weather years of economic depression and decline in between; he witnessed them go through many shapes and forms – turret and arch-decked, corrugated-hulled, three-island types and 'standard' types of both wars, the Doxford 'Economy' motorships of the 1930s, through to large, dry cargo bulk carriers.

Vessels galore. The Tyne at North Shields around 1910 was crowded with ships.

When he had begun his business life there had been about 60 tramp steamer owners with offices on Tyneside. At his death in 1968 they numbered less than ten. His own company, after various corporate transformations, disposed of their last ships in 1981.

In 1953, B.J. Sutherland & Co., another well-known Tyne tramp concern, had gone out of business after just over 60 years. This was largely due to the crippling £1.5m death duties levelled after the death of its head, Sir Arthur Munro Sutherland.

In 1967, Runciman's moved their operations to Glasgow and in the same year Stephens, Sutton's faded away. In 1974, Chapman's, after undergoing a name change to Chapman & Willan Ltd., was sold to the Burnett Steamship Company of Newcastle, established in 1891, which in turn only survived for another eight years. In 1979 Dalgliesh's left the shipping scene along with Hall Brothers who went into liquidation.

Finally, in 1983 Robinson's Stag Line sold its last ship, the Walker-built bulk carrier *Begonia*. Tramp owning on the Tyne had come to an end and so had a way of life for many seafarers.

Storm and rescue

The Tyne's sea links with Norway go back a long way. As early as the 1860s steamers were carrying passengers from Newcastle to the land of the fjords. Bergen and Trondheim in Western Norway featured as the main destinations of these ships, but in 1890 a passenger service was also begun to Christiania (Norway's capital, later renamed Oslo) on the eastern side of the country.

Also in 1890, the Bergen Steamship Company (known as the Bergen Line), in co-operation with the Northern Steamship Company of Trondheim and the firm of Peter Halvorsen, started running passenger steamers to Western Norway from the Tyne as part of an agreement to share the service between them.

However, in 1892 Peter Halvorsen's shipping business collapsed and the service to Western Norway continued under the joint operation of the Bergen and Northern companies, becoming known as the B&N Line. This arrangement lasted until after the First World War. Then, from late 1921, the Bergen Line found itself the sole operator of the link to Stavanger and Bergen after the Northern Steamship Company withdrew.

Many of the early ships on the passenger run to Bergen used the Albert Edward Dock, North Shields, as their departure and arrival point in the river. However, in 1913 the Bergen Line switched their berth to Newcastle Quayside which they used until the opening of the Tyne Commission Quay (also known as the Riverside Quay) at North Shields in 1928. The Bergen ships were then transferred to this new terminal.

The Fred Olsen Line, which had taken over the Oslo route in 1906, at first used Tyne Dock. Later, the company opened a berth at Newcastle Quayside which was used as well as the dock. Eventually, however, the Tyne Commission Quay would become the departure and arrival point of the Olsen vessels, a facility they shared with the Bergen Line.

NORWAY.  NORWAY.

WEEKLY COMMUNICATION BETWEEN

NEWCASTLE AND BERGEN,

By the FAST FIRST-CLASS NORWEGIAN ROYAL MAIL STEAMER

"NORGE,"

920 TONS GROSS REGISTER.   Captain F. WIESE.

FARES — £3 Single, £5 Return, Including all meals.

Leaves the TYNE every Tuesday at 7 o'clock P.M. Leaves BERGEN every Saturday at 9 o'clock P.M.

AVERAGE PASSAGE, 36 HOURS.

BORRIES, CRAIG & Co., Newcastle-on-Tyne,

C/129   Agents.

An advertisement of 1887 for the Norge which entered service in 1882.

The opening of the Tyne Commission Quay next to the Albert Edward Dock at North Shields in 1928 was a milestone in the history of the crossings to Norway. Through trains began operating direct from London via Newastle to the quay so that passengers could walk on to the ferries with little inconvenience and a considerable saving in time.

In 1931, a new Bergen Line passenger ship appeared at the Tyne Commission Quay. This handsome two-funnel vessel was named the *Venus*. She was the second of the company's ships with this name – it was the custom of the line to name its ferries after planets or stars. The first *Venus* had operated for many years on the Western Norway service but was now withdrawn.

The successful career of the second *Venus* plying between the Tyne and Bergen reached a dramatic climax in January 1937 when storm force winds, rising to hurricane force at times, amid a blizzard, turned the North Sea into an area of extreme danger.

As the *Venus* made her way from Bergen on passage to the Tyne she encountered formidable seas. Other, smaller ships, were out there in the vast expanse, battling against the waves to reach the shelter of a port. These vessels included the Norwegian cargo carrier *Trym*, of Trondheim, with a crew of 19 aboard. Heavy seas crashed relentlessly on to the ship, badly flooding the galley and engine room. The crew realised she was in danger of sinking.

But help was to arrive. The wireless operator of the *Venus* picked up the *Trym*'s SOS call via a coastal radio station, and her master, Captain Wilhelm Dreyer, ordered his vessel to sail to the rescue.

When he reached the stricken ship's position, the captain was unable to mount an immediate rescue attempt as night had fallen and the seas were too heavy. At one point the *Venus* even lost contact with the *Trym*, but eventually found her again.

The captain then called for volunteers to man a lifeboat. An attempt was to be made to save the *Trym*'s crew despite the appalling conditions. The response was overwhelming. Captain Dreyer found himself with too many volunteers. Only a handful of the *Venus*'s crew could be picked for a mission requiring great courage.

Amid the raging seas six men from the *Trym* were taken aboard the lifeboat which then returned to the rescue ship. This was made possible by the courage of *Trym* crew member Perry Opsahl who jumped into the water with a line and managed to reach the lifeboat. Five of his fellow crewmen were then brought to safety using a line and lifebuoy.

The youngest member of the *Trym*'s crew, 17-year-old Arne Ristan, was so exhausted he failed to grasp the ladder after the lifeboat came alongside the *Venus*. Arne fell into the sea and was washed under the lifeboat. However, someone managed to catch hold of him and haul him to safety. Briefly unconscious, he awoke to find himself on the deck of the *Venus*.

But the operation was not yet over. Thirteen other men still remained on the *Trym* as she was pounded by the huge waves. However, luck was to change the situation. A temporary lessening of the storm provided the *Venus* with her opportunity. Displaying expert seamanship, Captain Dreyer brought his vessel close to the stricken steamer.

After several attempts, the *Venus* managed to shoot a line across to the *Trym* by means of a rocket and the remainder of the crew were hauled the short distance through the rough seas to the safety of the *Venus*'s decks by means of a line and

The Norway Wharf at Newcastle Quayside, probably early in World War I. Alongside is the Bergen and Northern Line's Capella, which may have been on relief duties. Ferries were to sail to Bergen from this wharf until 1928 when the Tyne Commission Quay at North Shields was opened.

lifebuoy. The *Trym*'s men had been smashed against the sides of the ferry in the process, but all 19 were able to walk the deck of the rescue ship. Captain Torkildsen of the *Trym* was the last to leave his vessel.

The *Venus* pulled away from the sinking ship and sailed on towards the Tyne as she was violently assailed by the storm. The heavy seas smashed doors in the second-class compartments, causing flooding in one of the public rooms. Second-class passengers had to be moved to first-class accommodation after water seeped into their cabins. Two crew members were slightly injured and a lifeboat was swept away amid the ferocity of the storm.

All aboard must have been greatly relieved as the *Venus* entered the sheltered waters between the Tyne piers, not least of them the 19 lucky men from the *Trym*. Captain Dreyer was moved by the warm welcome he and his crew received from the people of Tyneside upon landing.

He told the *North Mail*: 'Watching the headquarters flag of the Tynemouth Volunteer Life Brigade dip in salute as we passed and seeing those hundreds of people gathered at the Commissioners' Quay I could not help but think to myself "So English". We rescued Norwegians but they treat us as though it had been Englishmen.' Some might add 'So Geordie' to the description 'So English'.

The *Venus*'s men had shown outstanding courage. He captain had displayed fine seamanship, patience and perseverance in the face of exceptionally hazardous conditions.

For his key role in the rescue, Captain Dreyer was made a Knight Commander of Norway's Order of St Olav and received the Silver Medal of Lloyds of London. The seamen who manned the lifeboat were not forgotten either. They were awarded the Norwegian Gold Medal for a Noble Deed.

Ordinary Seaman Perry Opsahl, of the *Trym*, received the same honour for his outstanding bravery in taking the line to the lifeboat.

Tyneside had its own appropriate award for Captain Dreyer. He was made an honorary member of the Tynemouth Volunteer Life Brigade.

During the Second World War the *Venus*, along with other Bergen Line ships, was seized by the Germans during their occupation of Norway. The ferry was used as a depot vessel for U-boats.

In April 1945, as the war approached its closing stages, the *Venus* was bombed by Allied aircraft as she lay moored in Hamburg harbour and sank to the bottom. However, the ship was to be reborn. After the war, a salvage operation was begun and she was raised from the harbour bed.

The *Venus* was then towed from Hamburg to Denmark, where she underwent a major reconstruction. She emerged from this rebuilding with two new funnels and a new bow section. The vessel was now able to carry more passengers. In 1948 the *Venus* was placed back on the Bergen-Newcastle run. It was a remarkable comeback. The ship did not go the breaker's yard until 1968.

Today, the Fjord Line operates a car and passenger ferry to Stavanger and Bergen from the Tyne, continuing a long-standing link to Western Norway. The DFDS shipping company, whose vessels are also well known in the river, runs a car and passenger ferry service to Kristiansand in South-Eastern Norway before sailing onwards to Gothenburg in Sweden. The terminal in the river for both these services, and for the DFDS ships to Amsterdam, is next to the original Tyne Commission Quay where the *Venus* berthed after her extraordinary rescue mission.

Venus arrives safely home at the Tyne Commission Quay,
North Shields, after her rescue mission in 1937.

Newcastle Chronicle & Journal Ltd.

A seafaring family: the Inches of North Shields

Many families on the Tyne have a long sea-faring history. Large numbers of men from the area served in sailing colliers, other merchant ships, and the Royal Navy. An example of one such sea-faring family is the Inch family of North Shields.

On 23 July 1824 Archibald Inch, a North Shields lad of 14, was apprenticed to Robert Bradshaw, shipowner and ropemaker. The boy's apprenticeship was to last for seven years during which time Robert Bradshaw undertook to *'teach, learn and inform him the said Apprentice, or cause him to be taught, learned and informed in the Art, Trade or Business of a Mariner or Seaman.'*

He would be paid £50 over the seven years, plus seven shillings in *'the winter season as the ships shall be laid up or unemployed in lieu of board and lodging'*. Archibald would provide for himself *'all manner of sea bedding … and other Necessaries'*.

Apprenticeships lasted until a boy was 21 regardless of how old he was when he started, so lads who got their training underway early were more experienced and more useful at 21 than those who started later.

The brig Rolling Wave, Archibald Inch Commander, at Port Venice in 1854. The ship, which was built in North Shields that year, was to founder in the Baltic in 1890. Captains could quickly purchase a 'portrait' of their ship in ports such as Venice as local painters kept stock samples of typical vessels and simply added the ship's name.

Archibald served his time and moved up though the ranks of seamanship. By 1854 he had become Master of the brig *Rolling Wave* which he commanded on her maiden voyage to Venice. He died in 1856 aged just 46, leaving a wife and two sons, John aged 17 and Archibald (II) aged 11.

John Inch and his brother were both apprenticed to shipowners and both did well. John served his apprenticeship on the brig *Symmetry* on the Quebec trade and at 21 was promoted to second mate. In 1866 the *Shields Gazette* noted there was cholera aboard *Victory*, the ship of which John Inch was then captain. One man had died and an apprentice was ill.

In 1894 John Inch's wife, Meggy, was to have the honour of launching a large steamer, the *Kurrachee*, at Howdon for its owner, R.S. Donkin. This was a brave investment for days when trade was depressed. When John died in 1897, aged 59, of a diseased liver ('the result of voyages in India and China'), his obituary noted that he was 'a perfect specimen of a bluff and honest seaman'. They had no children.

In 1868 John's younger brother, Archibald (II), aged 21 and out of his apprenticeship, was employed on *Balkan*, a 382-ton ship registered at North Shields. By 1871 he was mate on the barque *Canada West* on the run to Riga. That year he was certified Master.

He married in July 1872 and his bride, Isabel, a North

Captain Archibald Inch (II) relaxes with a pipe on board ship, probably the James Barrass, around 1890.

Shields seamstress, made a note in her accounts book: 'My Archie sailed' on 18 October. In June 1873 she notes that she has word of his safe arrival at Sydney and on 26 July she notes 'Had a letter from Archie by *Limerick*. Sailed for New York yesterday.' It could take many weeks for news to reach home. Isabel, like other seamen's wives, sailed with her husband several times.

By 1874 Archibald (II) was Chief Officer on the *Boadicea* on the Mediterranean and Indian trades (and was described as 'sober and steady'). That year he joined the *James Barrass* as Chief Officer, and stayed with her until 1893. His last ship was the SS *Timor*. From 1872 to 1895 he had been employed by Henry Adamson of Mercantile Chambers, Newcastle. He died in North Shields in 1912.

His only child was a daughter, Harriet, who married a ship's engineer, and, like her mother, had to get used to long separations. Her husband's letters survive and in one, written in 1906 from the SS *Bombay*, to his wife and baby son in North Shields, he laments that he has not had a Christmas at home since 1895. The only entertainment on board ship in the Indian Ocean that year was, he says, a rat hunt and a pillow fight: 'the competitors sat astride the boom and had to try to knock each other off with a pillow.'

A rowing boat makes for the landing stage at North Shields fish quay around 1900. On the shore the High Lights and the Low Lights stand out clearly. The lighthouses were built 1807-1810 as navigation beacons to help sailors coming into the treacherous mouth of the Tyne. When the lights lined up the passage was safe. The Low Light at around 100 feet tall is slightly taller than the High Light, further up the bank. The Scottish herring fleet are drying their high lugsails; soon steam drifters would take their place in the North Sea. Unloading at the dock is the Tyne Stream, which belonged to the Tyne Steam Fishing Co. Ltd. She was built in Middlesbrough in 1891.

A Tyne steam ferry, probably the Northumbrian, approaches North Shields ferry landing in 1969. By 1972 she had been replaced by a diesel vessel. There had been steam ferries between North and South Shields since 1827, run by various companies with varying success. The Direct Ferry or 'Ha'penny Dodger' (so called because of the way it weaved through river traffic) crossed for 107 years until it ceased in 1954. The ferries were vital but unpopular as they were unreliable and did not operate in fog, or at night. However, for many years, in some areas, only genuine travellers were entitled to buy a drink, so a return ferry ticket could provide useful proof of travel to show to the local publican!

Men of Shields

Among the most familiar sights of the Tyne were the foyboats and the men who manned them. The task of the foyboatmen was to moor ships on arrival in the river and to cast off the lines when they sailed. Familiar also were the pilots who guided vessels into and out of the river.

Ted Harle, who was born in South Shields where the pilots were based, has memories of when he lived on the town's Lawe Top as a boy from 1926 to 1936. This elevated area at the mouth of the river was home to many of the pilots and their families.

He told the authors: 'The people who lived on the Lawe Top were nearly all connected with the river in one way or another – the pilots, the foyboatmen and the shipyard workers. The pilots in particular were very prominent.

'The beach we frequented was the one between The Groyne and the pilot jetty. At the end of this jetty the pilot cutter was moored, and on the river side of the jetty were about six foyboats, which were very heavily built and painted black with a black and white border on the top.

'We would see ships coming in and as they got near The Groyne area they would slow up, but still keep steerage. Two foyboatmen would row out and it was a very frantic operation to row and pick up the rope, which was fastened on the ship from the bow to amidships and went in a loop down to about two or three feet in the water. The foyboatmen had to

row like mad to get to this rope, grab it and strap the foyboat to it. They were then carried upriver by the ship to wherever she was to berth and they would then take the ropes from the ship to tie the vessel up.

'I don't think I've ever seen this in any other port in the world. It was very interesting to watch. I never saw the foyboatmen make a mistake. After going up river with an inbound ship you would see them rowing back down to their base. They were big, tough characters and I think people respected them for the difficult job they did.'

Ted, who served as a radio officer with Royal Mail Lines, also remembers the long-standing Arab community at South Shields. This began in the decade before the First World War when Arab seamen from the Yemen and adjacent Aden Protectorate began arriving in the town. Their numbers increased during the First World War in which many served aboard British vessels with distinction.

These seamen, who sometimes included Somalis, were accommodated at Arab-run boarding houses in the town and would generally take up jobs as firemen on ships, carrying out the hot and arduous job of stoking and maintaining the coal-burning furnaces. Arab seamen, boarding-house keepers and shopkeepers sometimes married local women and today a considerable number of South Shields people are their descendants.

In the period between the two world wars there were

The pilot cutter Queen o' the May off the Coble Landing, South Shields, around 1932.

occasional disturbances and tensions between the British and Arab seafarers in the town mainly because of competition for jobs in the years of economic depression. These tensions culminated in a violent disturbance involving seamen in early August 1930 at the Mill Dam, where the men signed on for ships. It was dubbed a 'riot'.

After the Second World War, in which Arab crew members again put in excellent service for Britain, the Yemeni community was generally fully accepted by the people of South Shields, becoming a familiar part of the town's make-up. Indeed, there was considerable integration between the two communities and it is not unusual to find Shields people of mixed descent with Arab surnames.

Ted recalls: 'I went to Baring Street School, which was just beside the Roman fort. There were about half a dozen Arab boys in the class there with me. There were 50 or 60 in a class in those days, I suppose. They were very loyal members of the school. If the school was playing football away, they would be there.

'Many years later, I sailed with a cargo ship out of the Tyne called the *Holly Park* – one of Denholm's of Glasgow – and we had Yemeni Arab crewmen in the engine room and a Geordie crew on deck. We were away for two years and there was not a happorth of trouble. Wonderful – both groups were the best seamen in the world. We were two years running between Australia and New Zealand.'

The pilot boats were a constant feature of the Tyne. Ted recalls there was a pilot office on the Lawe Top in North Marine Park. 'They were in an excellent position there – they could see all the harbour. Pilots had to serve their time at sea and go deep sea to get their masters' tickets.

'Pilots on the Tyne were drawn from families such as the

Pilots on the Protector during her speed trials, October 1907.

Purvises, the Marshalls and Wrigglesworths. Some of them used to live quite close to us on the Lawe Top, Roman Road way, and other ones who were a bit more affluent lived in the Avenues, like Julian Avenue, which ran west to east from Lawe Road.'

In the earliest days the pilots used cobles, that distinctive boat of the north-eastern coast from Flamborough Head to Berwick. They would sail out of the Tyne, cruising up and down the coast 'seeking' ships bound for Shields.

However, in 1907 came a major change. In that year the system of using cobles and 'seeking' ships was replaced by a steam-driven pilot cutter, the *Protector*. She was a substantial one-funnel vessel which took pilots out to ships waiting to enter the Tyne and also took pilots off departing ships when they reached the sea. The 110-ft long *Protector* had been built at South Shields by J.P. Rennoldson's yard for the Tyne Pilotage Commissioners.

The pilot cutter Protector. *She was to meet a tragic end during World War I.*

Sadly, her career was ended during the First World War after only nine years of service. Early on 31 December 1916 the *Protector* was hit by major tragedy. She struck a mine as she was preparing to put a pilot on board the collier *Mile End* some distance outside the Tyne piers. The crew of the *Mile End* felt the powerful explosion, which was followed by a great pall of smoke. The *Protector* immediately sank and all 19 men aboard were killed, probably instantly. The mine had been laid by a U-boat.

Those who lost their lives were ten pilots, four pilots' assistants and five crew. Eight of the pilots and pilots' assistants were from South Shields and two from North Shields. All the crew members lived at North Shields. Three of the 19 were aged under 20, and the youngest, an assistant steward, was a boy aged 15.

Pilots at South Shields watch house in North Marine Park scan the horizon for ships in need of their services, around 1946.

A tablet in memory of the 19 is sited in St Stephen's Church on the Lawe Top. It was erected by the Tyne Pilotage Authority and features a relief showing the *Protector* as well as the names of those who died.

In earlier years there had been great dangers for mariners

in peacetime as well as wartime at the river mouth. South Shields is the birthplace of the first purpose-built lifeboat, The *Original*, and the town's pilots played a key role in the early lifeboat service when shipwreck was a frequent occurrence.

Sailing colliers and other vessels were often driven on to the stretch of coast at the river entrance by storms or gales. They might end up on the Herd Sand at South Shields or hit the treacherous Black Middens rocks off Tynemouth. Ships could also come to grief in the turbulent, shallow waters of the Tyne Bar, a ridge of sand and shingle stretching across the river entrance.

In 1789 the collier *Adventure* was wrecked on the Herd Sand during a strong gale. The ship was only a few hundred yards from the beach but the sea was so rough that Shields boatmen were unable to attempt a rescue. Seven of the *Adventure*'s crew, plus the captain, were lost. A crowd of people gathered on the beach, helpless to intervene because of that fateful few hundred yards of raging sea. Some of the unfortunate crewmen clung to the rigging but then fell into the waves.

The tragedy which befell this ship and other vessels at the river mouth led to the development of the first purpose-built lifeboat. The *Adventure* disaster had spurred a social group of South Shields businessmen and others – known as the 'Gentlemen of Lawe House' – to start a fund and hold a competition with a prize of two guineas for the best designed rescue vessel. The result was *The Original*.

The 'Gentleman of Lawe House' set up a committee which recommended that the craft should be of considerable buoyancy with an identical bow and stern so that the boat did not have to turn around in heavy seas. They indicated that both bow and stern should be high to keep out the sea as much as possible, and the boat should be of shallow draught. The committee therefore stipulated the fundamental concepts.

There has been much controversy over who invented this boat. Both William Wouldhave, a house painter and parish clerk of St Hild's, South Shields, and Henry Greathead, a boatbuilder, put forward designs and other men also suggested ideas. Wouldhave even built a tin model boat which featured air boxes for buoyancy and he is also believed to have suggested cork as an alternative material for the same pur-

South Tyneside MBC

The first purpose-built lifeboat, The Original. She carried out her first rescue on 30 January 1790.

A detail from 'The Invention of the Lifeboat, Willie Wouldhave', by Ralph Hedley.

pose. The tin model had a high canoe-like bow and stern which were identical.

Greathead's craft was said to be flat-bottomed and did not apparently feature air boxes or cork. But the committee rejected both Wouldhave and Greathead's designs as not being quite right and so there was no winner of the two-guinea prize.

Despite this, they offered Wouldhave one guinea – half the prize – a possible indication of their admiration for his efforts and ingenuity. Or was that offer a sign that they had been influenced by his model or ideas and wished to give him some recompense? It is impossible to give a definite answer. Wouldhave's probable idea of cork for buoyancy was adopted, though it was almost certainly not a new one.

Nicholas Fairless and Michael Rockwood, two leading members of the committee, produced a clay model from which, they said, the actual vessel was built. Although 'The Gentlemen of Lawe House' took into account Wouldhave and Greathead's proposals they also assessed ideas from a number of other men. These may have included principles used by Lionel Lukin, who had converted vessels for lifesaving a few years earlier. What emerged was a mixture of concepts from various sources which went towards creating *The Original*. It seems therefore that no one person invented the first purpose-built lifeboat.

One fact is beyond doubt, Henry Greathead was given the job of building the vessel, but this was under the direction of the committee. In addition, he was to be awarded £1,200 by Parliament, which officially recognised him as the inventor, a move which has only served to fuel the controversy.

As built, *The Original* had relatively high, pointed bows and stern, a layer of cork along the sides both inside and out for buoyancy, a clinker-built overlapping wood design, sturdy construction and, at the suggestion of Greathead, a curved keel to aid manoeuvrability. It seems that Wouldhave, with his idea of cork, and

Henry Greathead, one of the key figures in the creation of The Original.

Greathead, with his curved keel and construction know-how, both made a valuable contribution.

The Original, which was oar-pulled, saved several hundred lives during a long career between 1790 and 1830. This pioneering craft carried out her first rescue on 30 January 1790, when she saved the crew of a vessel driven on to the Herd Sand, the place where the *Adventure* had met disaster the previous year.

William Wouldhave had recommended that the lifeboat should be built of copper to prevent her tearing on rocks, an idea which was rejected. It was ironic therefore that *The Original*'s career was ended when the wooden-hulled craft was damaged on rocks. However, by that time she had proved her worth in many rescues.

Other pioneering lifeboats based at the mouth of the river, such as the *Northumberland* and the *Tyne*, put in sterling work too. The South Shields-based *Tyne* saved more than 1,000 lives between 1833 and 1877. The North Shields-based *Northumberland*, built by Greathead, also notched up an excellent rescue record.

The Shields lifeboats were manned by the Tyne pilots. They were the natural

The lifeboat Tyne at the Coble Landing, South Shields, c.1858. She saved over 1,000 lives.

men for the job because they knew local waters intimately. But the pilots, who displayed great courage, were not immune from danger. This was tragically illustrated in December 1849 when the lifeboat *Providence* capsized. Twenty of her 24-man crew were drowned. She had been on her way to rescue the crew of the *Betsy*, of Littlehampton. Those lost are commemorated, like the men of the *Protector*, in St Stephen's Church.

Today, the *Tyne* lifeboat is the centrepiece of The Lifeboat Memorial in Ocean Road, South Shields, which commemorates both Wouldhave and Greathead. The town honours both men who endeavoured to save lives through their practical ideas.

As well as a history of rescue on the waves, South Shields is a community with a very strong seafaring tradition. Its Marine School was founded in 1861 to provide education in navigation and astronomy. A purpose-built home for the school was opened in Ocean Road in 1869 and in 1903 a marine engineering department was started. Thousands of seamen have been trained at the school which still operates today as a department of South Tyneside College.

Perhaps unsurprisingly, large numbers of the town's men have served in the Merchant Navy, many putting in magnificent service during the Second World War. Sadly, a large number were also lost in that war. Indeed, more merchant seamen from South Shields died in the conflict than from any other town in Britain. Today, a memorial to the thousands of Merchant Navy men who sailed from the port and lost their lives in the war stands at the Mill Dam. It takes the form of a statue depicting a seafarer at a ship's wheel, facing the river. The memorial was unveiled in 1990.

The Mill Dam is now a much quieter place. Sightseers and Customs House theatre-goers have replaced the men who once congregated there to sign on for ships, and the nearby Harton Staiths, with their coal-cascading spouts and dusty collier ships, have disappeared.

Only yards away from the Merchant Navy statue, the Tyne, wide at this point, flows inexorably to the North Sea. The coaly river is no longer coaly and salmon grace its restless, ever stirring waters.

South Tyneside MBC

The tug Plover with the German five-masted barque RC Rickmers in tow before World War I.

Lifeboats including Bedford, Tom Perry and Willie Wouldhave at the National Pilots' Conference, May 1913. On the Tyne, the lifeboats were generally crewed by the pilots.

Some sources consulted

Periodicals

Amateur Photography
Marine News
Lloyds Register of Shipping
Lloyd's Casualty Returns
Mercantile Navy List
Nautical Magazine
Sea Breezes
Shipbuilding and Shipping Record
Smith's Dock Journal
Tyne Improvement Commission Handbooks
The Young Men's Magazine

Newspapers

Newcastle Daily Journal
Newcastle Evening Chronicle
Newcastle Mail
Newcastle Journal & North Mail
North Mail
Newcastle Weekly Chronicle
Northern Weekly Leader
The Times

Books

History of the Football Association (London, 1953).
A.G. Course, *The Merchant Navy* (London, 1963).
R.E. Keys, *Dictionary of Tyne Sailing Ships* (Newcastle, 1998).
Frank Manders & Richard Potts, *Crossing the Tyne* (Tyne Bridge Publishing, 2001).
J. Lingwood & H. Appleyard, *Chapman of Newcastle* (Kendal, 1985).
J. Lingwood & L. Gray, *Stephens, Suttons Limited* (Kendal, 1983).
N.L. Middlemiss, *Travels of the Tramps*, Vols I to IV (Newcastle, 1989-1993).
N.L. Middlemiss, *Black Diamond Fleets* (Newcastle, 2000).
A.M. Northway, 'The Tyne Steam Shipping Co.', article in *Maritime History*, Volume II. Robert Craig, ed. (Newton Abbot, 1973).
A.G. Osler, *Mr Greathead's Lifeboats* (Tyne & Wear Museums, 1990).
John H. Proud, *One Hundred and Fifty Years of the Maltese Cross* (Tyne & Wear Tugs Ltd., South Shields, 1993).
N.J. Robinson, *Stag Line and Joseph Robinson and Sons* (Kendal, 1984).
W. Runciman, *Before the Mast – And After* (London, 1924).

Paddle tug Titan off the Tyne around 1900. Note her tall 'bell-topped' funnels. She was built in Aberdeen in 1865 as Atlas, changed her name to Titan in 1873, and was bought by J. Batey and Son of Newcastle in 1888 (their house flag flies from her mast). She was broken up in 1936 at Dunston. Beyond Titan are an inward bound steamer and a deep-laden barquentine being towed seaward by a smoke-belching paddle tug.

Index of ships

Index of people mentioned

Select index of firms mentioned

Detail from the photograph
featured on page 68.